Poet Power

The Complete Guide to Getting Your Poetry Published

D0062587

Thomas A. Williams

SENTIENT PUBLICATIONS, LLC

First Sentient Publications edition 2002

Printed in Canada

Cover design by Kim Johansen, Black Dog Design

Book design by Thomas A. Williams

Library of Congress Cataloging-in-Publication Data

Williams, Thomas A. (Thomas Andrew), 1931-
  Poet Power : the complete guide to getting your poetry pub-
lished / Thomas A. Williams.– 1st Sentient Publications ed.
    p. cm.
Includes index.
 ISBN 1-59181-002-7
 1. Poetry–Marketing. I. Title.
 PN1059.M3 W55 2002
 808.1–dc21

2002011178

SENTIENT PUBLICATIONS

A Limited Liability Company
1113 Spruce Street
Boulder, CO 80302
www.sentientpublications.com

For my girls:
Andrea and Lisa,
Madeleine, Anna, and Currin

Also by Thomas A. Williams

Mallarmé and the Language of Mysticism
Eliphas Lévi: Master of Occultism
The Bicentennial Book
We Choose America
Tales of the Tobacco Country
How to Publish Your Poetry
Publish Your Own Magazine, Guide Book,
or Weekly Newspaper
How to Publish Weekly Newspapers and
Free Circulation Shoppers
How to Publish City and Regional Magazines
The Query Letter That Never Fails
The Self-Publisher's Handbook of Contacts and Sources
How to Make $100,000 a Year in Desktop Publishing

The lunatic, the lover and the poet
Are of imagination all compact:
One sees more devils than vast hell can hold.
That is the madman. The lover, all as frantic
Sees Helen's beauty in a brow of Egypt.
The poet's eye, in fine frenzy rolling
Doth glance from heaven to earth, from earth
      to heaven
And as imagination bodies forth
The forms of things unknown, the poet's eye
Turns them into shapes, and gives to airy nothing
A local habitation and a name.

—William Shakespeare
A Midsummer Night's Dream

Contents

by Piece • How to Prepare a Media Kit • How and Where to Send Review Copies • The Power of News Releases, and How to Write Them • How to Get on Television and What to Do Once You Get There.

Find Them • Selling Through Catalogues • Premium and Promotional Sales of Your Books

Preface

"You ought really to try to sleep, Porphyro,
even though in this town poetry's a
bedroom occupation."

Hart Crane wrote these lines during a time when he had been exiled to Akron, Ohio to work in one of the stores belonging to his father's business, the Crane Chocolate Company. As a poet he felt utterly isolated. There was no one around in that provincial city even to read his poetry, let alone talk about it.

Almost every serious writer can identify with Crane's feelings. Writing can often seem a lonely, isolating, totally private occupation, especially when the things we write remain unpublished and unknown to others, filed away in desk drawers, private diaries, and notebooks—a "bedroom occupation."

So long as our words remain private to us, they are incomplete and inert. Power is generated only when the work is published—proclaimed to the public. And there are certainly few things more important than to proclaim the work of the poet to the public. Without poetry—the most intensely focused and personal art—we all remain finally separated from one another. With it, we can begin at least to know one another, from the inside out.

—*Tom Williams*
Savannah, Georgia

Chapter One / The Enterprise of Poetry

The act of publishing is as important to our poetic enterprise as the act of writing. Poets are preeminently tellers of truth: truth about themselves and others, truth about living together on this earth, truth about life, death, and destiny. Today, the world desperately needs truth tellers. That is why it is both desirable and a clear duty that the poets among us not only give voice to their insights but publish them for others to share.

Yet, of all writers, poets have the most difficulty getting their words into print. That's why *Poet Power* is an eminently practical book, nothing less than a how-to guide to the real world of publishing. It leaves to you the difficulty of writing the poem itself: getting the words right, the images right, and the rhythms right. It deals with another world, one that most poets do not know their way around in: the hard-nosed world of publishing and bookselling. If you want to get published, *Poet Power* will tell you, step-by-step, what you must do to achieve your sought-after goal.

What You Will Learn

The pages which follow contain an organized approach to the marketing of poetry that anyone can adopt and follow. When you do you will be amazed at the results. Here's what you will learn:

- You will learn what you need to know to build a successful career as a poet.
- You will learn methods that will help you place your poems in magazines and other periodicals regularly.
- You will learn how to interest publishers in bringing out your poems in book form.
- You will learn how to take your future into your own hands and successfully publish and market your work for yourself.

Faulkner, on the Poet's Duty

I believe that man will not merely endure: he will prevail. He is immortal, not because he alone among creatures has an inexhaustible voice, but because he has a soul, a spirit capable of compassion and sacrifice and endurance. The poet's, the writer's, duty is to write about these things. It is his privilege to help man endure by lifting his heart, by reminding him of the courage and honor and hope and pride and compassion and pity and sacrifice which have been the glory of his past. The poet's voice need not merely be the record of man, it can be one of the props, the pillars to help him endure and prevail.

—William Faulkner, *The Nobel Prize Address*

- You will even learn how to set up your own small publishing company to publish not only your own work but the work of other poets as well.
- You will learn how to become the editor of your own poetry series.
- You will learn how to sell your books once they are published.
- You will learn how to enhance your reputation as a published poet to achieve worthwhile goals and become a spokesperson for poetry—and all the arts—in your community.

There Is Much to Learn from Non-Fiction Writers

The successful writer of non-fiction magazine articles understands from the beginning that to be a good writer is not enough. He understands that, in addition to mastering the craft of writing, he has to learn to become a master marketer of his own work. He carefully and painstakingly studies market trends and needs. He studies the art of writing query letters and book outlines. He keeps these outlines and queries in circulation relentlessly until he strikes pay-dirt. He establishes a specialty and cultivates a group of magazines and magazine editors who are interested in the kind of thing that he has to say.

> The feeling that the systematic selling of one's product is somehow beneath the dignity of the poet is a widespread attitude, and it is a dreadfully self-defeating one. It is both desirable and a clear duty that the poets among us not only give voice to their insights but publish them for others to share.

Moreover, to the degree that he is successful the non-fiction writer will have learned to be persistent—very persistent. He doesn't stop trying to sell an article idea until he has systematically exhausted all publication possibilities. He understands that sooner or later, if he just keeps at it, there will be fortuitous matching of his idea and a publisher's immediate need. And when that happens the result is very happy indeed: publication and a check in the mail.

And, if he is not successful in placing his book, he may well elect to

A Peculiar Bias, Indeed

[There has been] a very peculiar bias...that is only now beginning to erode. This is the sense that publishing a book is an act somehow outside the main avenues of commerce; that people who deal with ideas should not sully themselves with such crass concerns as salesmanship, advertising, market share—with finding, in fact, an audience for what the writer...has so laboriously created.

—Robert A. Carter, in *Trade Book Marketing*

publish it himself, bringing it to bookstore shelves bearing the imprint of his own, newly-formed publishing company. That, in fact, is just what I did with this very book. The new technologies of desktop publishing, fax machines, and telecommunications have brought an absolute revolution in the publishing business. As the big publishing houses founder, the independent presses—often one or two person shops—are thriving, and the ambitious non-fiction writer has no hesitation at all in joining this wave of change and progress.

Poets Take Note

Poets who use these same techniques and adopt these same attitudes can and will be published, too. Yet few seem really to do so. The feeling that the systematic selling of one's product is somehow beneath the dignity of the poet is a widespread attitude, and it is a dreadfully self-defeating one. It certainly is not one shared by some very great poets. Walt Whitman, the greatest American poet of all, was a tireless self-promoter.

The famous public readings given in our own day by such poets as Dylan Thomas were not only literary events but masterpieces of promotion and marketing. They generated newspaper articles and stories and accounted for a generous portion of the sales of his books. Thomas was a very fine poet, but it was the marketing of his work as much as the quality of it that made it sell to such a wide public.

Allen Ginsburg, whose poem "Howl" was one of the most important of his generation, became widely read due in large part to a natural gift for self-promotion. The powerful public persona he created for himself produced thousands of pages of newspaper, magazine, and book articles. The great success of this one poem became the cornerstone of an entire literary career.

Not all self-marketing is as flamboyant and aggressive as that of Ginsburg. It must, after all, grow out of the personality of the poet. Quite impressive regional reputations have been built on the simple willingness of poets to seek and fulfill assignments such as participating in "poets in the schools programs," giving readings at community colleges, appearing on local talk shows, and achieving and maintaining high visibility in regional arts and literary organizations.

Poet Power

Remember: Opportunity doesn't knock, you do. If the opportunity to publish your poetry is what you want, you have to locate it, seek it out, confidently approach it, and beat the door down, if necessary, until the way to it is clear.

Chapter Two / A Poet's Crash Course in the Economics of Publishing

What is going on in the office and in the mind of the publisher or editor on whose desk the postman deposits your packet of poems? The answer to this question is basic to your publishing strategy, and to help you understand it I hereby offer this Poet's Crash Course in the Economics of Publishing.

Until you truly comprehend and accept the rules of the game, you will be like a player who has devoted his life to fruitlessly trying to win a game whose rules he does not understand. And that, my friends, is quite a handicap.

The first, and most important rule of the game is simply this: *publishing is a business.* The corollary to this rule is that what gets published is most often what is good for business. Like the professional in any other business, the goal of the publisher is to make a profit and stay in business. People who work as publishers use these profits to buy groceries, pay the rent, and send the children off to college, just like the rest of us. They also use these profits to publish more books like yours.

A Risky Business

Publishing is a risky business. I became a publisher because I loved the business, and I suspect that many if not most publishers—especially in the smaller houses—share that motivation. Why else would they set out on such a perilous occupation? Pitfalls and dangers beset the unwary publisher on every side. The opportunity for financial loss is every bit as great—and usually greater—than the chance of gain.

The successful publisher truly lives by his wits. He guesses which books are likely to find favor with the reading public, which books are likely to build the reputation of his press, and he publishes them. He

The Two Worlds of Publishing

There are two worlds of publishing, separate and distinct. As a poet you will be dealing with both of them. The first is the world of consumer magazines and trade book publishing. The second is the "small press" world of chapbooks, literary reviews, and ephemeral, low-budget periodicals.

The publications that populate these worlds cater to different clienteles, and a poem that is perfect for one will not be acceptable at the other. Even such widely read occasional poems as the one Maya Angelou composed for the presidential inauguration of Bill Clinton or James Dickey's poem celebrating the first moon landing would not be welcomed into the pages of the more avant garde and experimental publications.

But, as different as these two worlds are, they have much in common. The poet still has to understand and satisfy editorial needs and expectations. *Writer's Digest* magazine publishes what it considers to be entertaining verse about "the writing life." Humorous poets like Richard Armour and Ogden Nash were welcomed even into the pages of the *New Yorker*, where name recognition and a certain sophistication go far toward satisfying editorial needs. This magazine and others, like the *Atlantic Monthly*, also publish more serious verse. Writer's guidelines from both insist that poets study the magazine before submitting and warn that they are not "break-in" markets for unknowns just now knocking at the door.

Editorial requirements are just as rigid in the little presses as in the publications of mass circulation. Editors of both literary and popular publications must meet the expectations of their readers. Their success depends on it.

decides which articles are likely to interest the readers of his magazine and he buys them. He is often on the lookout for specialty items, including poems, that will be meaningful to his specific readership and he buys these, too.

In making these decisions, the publisher/editor relies on his intuition and experience. If he misjudges too often, there is no profit—no groceries, no rent, no college tuition for the kids. Hence, since no one can afford to stay in a business that doesn't bring in enough money to live on, there is no longer a publisher.

Those Free Enterprise Twins: Risk and Profit

The free enterprise system is built on the twin pillars of risk and profit. You risk what you have—money, time, talent—in the hope of gaining far more than you risk. But it doesn't always work. In this way, it is a little like a loaded shotgun. The trusty, old double barrel can be used to hunt for game and stock the family larder. But misjudge a step and stumble, and that same reliable tool can shoot your foot off.

> *The reputation of a small, literary press is its stock-in-trade. It is built on the sheer artistic merit of the books it chooses to publish. Foundation grants and institutional subsidies depend on this reputation.*

I go into all this so that you, as a poet, can put yourself for a moment into the editor's or publisher's shoes. For them, everything is always at risk. As they practice their profession, they stand to make a profit. But they also may shoot themselves in the foot. This really smarts, and most publishers will do everything they can to avoid having it happen to them.

Most of us literary types don't really understand—or perhaps just don't think about—the risk/profit basis of business in general and the publishing business in particular. Before I became a publisher, I was a college professor. If I taught well, there was a check at the end of the month. If I taught badly, there was a check at the end of the month. When I didn't teach all summer long, there was still a check at the end of the month. My financial reward for the work I was doing was not directly related to the level of success I had achieved in it. The good fairy might as well have put my money in the departmental mailbox.

And then... I resigned my tenured professorship to become a publisher.

It was quite a revelation, as abrupt and sudden a reality bath as anyone has ever taken. When I performed badly, I got no check. The good fairy had taken a permanent leave of absence. Moreover, I had to pay out some of the money I had already received to cover current overhead and keep the doors open. If I took time off, I did not get paid. And no matter how well business was going at any given time, there lurked in the background the cold, sobering, all-too-true knowledge that things could (and would) go awry whenever they took a notion to do so. A book could bomb. Subscriptions could fall off. Postal rates could rise and eat up my profits. A competitor could come into the arena and dilute my market share ruinously. Or my building could burn down, or I could have a heart attack and not be able to continue in business.

Obviously I was betting that more good things than bad would happen to me and, on balance, this has been true. But it took constant attention and alertness to market opportunities and danger signals to bring this result about. Even in the best of times I was—and still am—constantly aware that every decision I make about what I accept for publication affects me and my business directly, as well as the well-being of those who depend on me. These basic human realities constitute the everyday furnishings of every editor's office, right along with the desk, the chair, and the word-processing computer. And it is into this office that your poems arrive, unsolicited.

Most of the magazines, journals, chapbooks, and other periodicals that publish poetry are brought out by relatively small companies that, in order to stay in business, must watch their finances closely. But even they are not the only ones at risk. Bigger fish are in harm's way as well. I once heard an enthusiastic young editor/publisher describe the start-up that he was then involved in. He gave us a detailed plan for the publication of his new *Southern Magazine*. The idea was that a magazine with a focus on the South, a new journalism style, and an aggressive editorial policy, in the style of *Texas Monthly* or *Esquire*, would generate subscriptions and advertising sales sufficient to turn a profit. The project was not under-financed. There was five million dollars in operating capital in the bank. The articles in the magazine proved to be first rate. Yet, within three years, the project ran out of gas. The five million was gone, and advertising revenues were not producing adequate cash flow to produce the hoped-for profit. The originating editor's name disappeared from the masthead. The magazine was sold to another company and its name and character were changed.

Publishing Magazines: A Financial Tightrope Act

Profits are slim in the magazine business. Most magazines operate on the tiniest of profit margins. They barely manage to produce the positive cash flow that enables them to stay in business. And even this is often accomplished by paying editors, artists, and especially writers (as you well know) as little money as possible—sometimes nothing at all.

Subscription and single copy (newsstand) sales of almost all magazines do not return a profit. Selling subscriptions by mail is expensive. Few readers renew their subscriptions automatically. To get them to do so requires an additional series of mailings. In fact, cash received from subscription sales and newsstand sales is barely adequate to support the cost of subscriber maintenance and the high cost of mailing out the magazines themselves.

Thus, when the editor reads through your submissions, he will have very important questions in his mind in addition to the one about the quality of your writing. Assuming that your poem is well written, he will ask himself such questions as these:

- Will my readers understand this poem?
- Will my readers like this poem and react positively to it?
- Will this poem pull its weight in creating positive reader reactions to my magazine?
- Is its subject matter in keeping with the editorial slant of my magazine?
- Is the poet someone whose name my readers will recognize

and react positively to?

- Can I do more for my magazine by using this poem than I can by putting something else in the same space?
- Does this poem interest *me*? (In the case of little magazines—and even the prestigious, small circulation reviews—the editor may well have hobbyhorse preferences that don't necessarily show up in the writer's guidelines he or she furnishes.)

Publishing in Book Form

It is difficult under any circumstances for an unknown poet to find a publisher for a book of verse. Without requisite marketing skills and a clear understanding of the economics of book publishing it is virtually impossible. The reason is simple. With very few exceptions, books of poetry do not make any money.

Here's the way book publishing works. The publisher brings out a paperback book of verse. He can sell it, at the most, for $10. Since he has learned that even the best verse does not sell very well, he has printed no more than 1000 copies and very likely—especially in the case of a small press—just 500. This means that he does not realize any economy of scale in the manufacture of his books. As a result, the production cost per copy of the book is relatively high. If the publisher knows his stuff and gets the best prices available, he can get the 500 copies printed and bound for, say, $1500, or $3 a book. He will have paid a typesetter 300 or so dollars. He has paid someone to lay the book out and ready it for printing. He has office overhead, billing expenses, and distribution expense. An artist will earn an additional $200 for a cover design. The publisher then pays the bookstores and wholesalers who sell his book at least 50% of the cover price and sometimes more. Thus, if he sells every copy available to him for sale (450, since 50 will have been mailed out for review) he will gross $4500.

- Of that $4500 he pays his retailers their 50% discount, leaving him $2250.
- Of that $2250 he will lose $250 to bad debts and spoilage, leaving $2000.
- Yet he has paid the printer $1500, the typesetter $300, the

cover artist $200. He will allow 10% of the gross for general office expense and overhead. All of this totals $2450. The result: in the best of all possible worlds, the publisher loses $450 on a book of poems even when he successfully sells every available copy of the first edition.

So why do some books of verse get published in spite of these discouraging facts?

- Sometimes the publisher is publicly supported, as is the case with a university press or a not-for-profit corporation, or has grant money to subsidize publication.
- Sometimes the publisher, who has other projects on which he is making money, brings out a book of verse for the love of it. I have done this myself. But you, as a poet, can't count on it. It doesn't happen every day.
- Sometimes (and this is more and more often the case, even with small presses and university presses of high reputation) the poet contributes to the expense of publication.
- Sometimes the poet has a reputation for giving successful readings and for self-promotion, thereby convincing the publisher that an edition of a thousand or more copies can be sold and that he can at least break even on the project.

You Can Beat the Odds

Bear in mind that while the publisher is devoting time and energy on your book of poems he is not doing the other things on which he depends for his livelihood. These are the facts, the rules of the game. If you think that they stack the odds against you, you are absolutely right. Too many writers—and not just poets—do not really understand how publishing works, and, as a result, live in a fantasy world that has little to do with the realities of the publishing marketplace. And that's what it is: a marketplace. That's the bad news. The good news is that these odds can be beaten when you accept the world as it is and develop a plan for finding your publishing niche within it.

On Publishing and Proclaiming

A poet who doesn't have a book of his own along to take orders on when he's giving a reading isn't a serious poet, because he doesn't really want to share his work with the people who come in contact with it. Every poet should therefore always have a book which he can take orders for, either by himself or via a friend by the entrance table. . . . Remember, the old meaning of "publish" is "proclaim." Well, proclaim then. If you have something to say or to show, say it or show it to all who will listen. That, not false modesty, is real professionalism.

—Dick Higgins
Something Else Press

Chapter Three / Nine Secrets of Publishable (and Readable) Poetry

From an editor's point of view, what makes poetry publishable? It is tempting to say that poetry that is very, very good and very powerful is publishable, but that may not necessarily be the case. It *is* true that the very best poems written are *worthy* of publication and *ought to be* published. But it does not follow that they *will* be published. The history of literature is filled with the names of great poets who had great difficulty getting their work before the public. Of course, we know the names only of those who ultimately succeeded in doing so. One wonders how many others there are whose work never did see the light of day.

Those who write at the highest level of achievement in every genre are exceedingly rare. I scarcely need to point out that not every American novelist is a Faulkner or a Hemingway, nor every poet a Walt Whitman or a Wallace Stevens. The rest of us—with lesser but still very valuable achievements—must study the available market for novels and poems and send our work where it is most likely to find acceptance.

A survey of the field quickly reveals the kinds of subject matter, style, and treatment that promise success. As editor and publisher of a regional magazine and owner of an independent book publishing company, I have read many submissions by poets anxious for publication. Some of these submissions I accepted, even though my magazine did not normally use poetry. Most I returned to the author with thanks and a letter of rejection that was as kind and thoughtful as I could make it.

Sometimes a good poem was returned to the author because there was simply no room for it in the foreseeable future. More often poems were returned because the poems did not embody all or most of the nine characteristics that would have made them publishable in my magazine or some other periodical of general circulation.

Check your own work against the list provided here. The more of

15

The Wide World of Poetry

The world of poetry is a very large one, and there is room in it for all of us. For some of the greatest poets, the act of putting words on paper is an attempt to capture the very meaning of life itself. Hart Crane wanted to utter the "perfect cry" that would "string some constant harmony." Mallarmé wanted to recreate in his verse the language of the "constellations themselves." T.S. Eliot created an immensely powerful and unforgettable image of the soul state of post-Copernican, existentially desolate man. Spiritual realities sweep through the poems of Wordsworth like an implacable rhythm through a symphony of Mozart.

Others of us give voice, in deeply personal ways, to every facet of the human condition, from the most profound and complex to the simplest and most direct.

Everyday life has its beauties too, as the work of little-known poets like Billie Varner, whom I talk about in the following pages, shows us so well. Michelangelo held up a mirror to man in his Sistine ceiling, but so did Grandma Moses in her rural landscapes. They both bring us joy.

And then there are the occasional poems, the celebratory poems, and the witty, humorous poems that make us laugh. They all have their place and their value. I will confess that even a greeting card verse once brought tears to my eyes when I read some particularly moving lines in a Father's Day card given to me by my young daughters. And then there are all those poems written in the middle of the night for ourselves alone.

Through poetry, we open ourselves to one another, and at whatever level this takes place, it is a very good thing indeed.

these publishing features you incorporate into your work, the more effectively you will be able to stake your claim to the limited space that is available for poetry at any given time.

1. On some level your poem must be immediately accessible to the general, intelligent reader.

The editor who is evaluating your poem will ask himself: will my readers understand and appreciate this verse? If there is any question at all in his mind, your work will be returned to you with a rejection slip.

The more clear and direct your work is the more likely it is to be accepted. As an editor I often enjoyed parts of poems that I nevertheless rejected because of the obscure personal references they contained—allusions to events or persons important to the poet but unlikely to be recognized or appreciated by others.

> *[A poet is] a writer and nothing else: a man alone in a room with the English language, trying to get human feelings right....*
> —*John K Hutchins*

This is a more general problem than you may think. I once wrote a poem that was built around another powerful image from my childhood. I had stood on the back porch of our South Georgia farmhouse and watched while my mother vainly struggled to keep a weeping willow tree safe from hurricane winds. The harder she fought, the more apparent it became to me that she would fail. And she did. This little drama came to embody for me the feeling that we are always at the mercy of forces far greater than our power to withstand them, and to which we must always give in. The poem failed, of course, because this association with willows was wholly personal. The image of the willow could not possibly engender in others the same strong feelings as it did in me.

Such private symbols, for all the power they may exert on us personally, cannot be understood by others. The public use of wholly private symbolism just does not work. Art itself may very well exist as a wholly private enterprise, but successful art, with its goal of communicating our vision to as many of our fellow men as possible, is always public.

Many poems are made virtually inaccessible to the general reader by the number of intellectual, literary, and philosophical allusions they contain. I have observed that poets who are also college teachers (and there are many of these, since teaching has become a favorite means of supporting the writing habit) often fall into this kind of poetical self-indulgence. Either they are simply writing for each other—a very restricted readership, indeed—or they are writing private verses for their private pleasure.

It takes a very great and very powerful poet to get away with such obscurities. There are, indeed, poems whose mere rhythms and words cause our hair to stand on end. But, even in these cases, we read the poems not because of the obscurities but in spite of them. The unmistakable power of the opening lines of Eliot's *The Waste Land* made the chore of dealing with the literary and anthropological puzzles and obscurities in the remainder of the text worthwhile and even necessary for me.

Fortunately, it is possible to write poetry of the very highest quality that is readily accessible to the general reader, although it may contain level upon level of deeper and deeper meaning. I think of poets as diverse as Dante, François Villon, Charles Baudelaire, and Robert Frost. No one would call this poetry superficial, yet it is readily accessible to any reader that comes upon it. The door is easily opened—although, once inside, not every reader will explore or be capable of exploring every room, every nook and cranny from attic to basement.

When I was a boy, I thought Frost's *Birches* was a poem about ice storms, and I was very satisfied with it that way. I read Dante almost as science fiction or fantasy. But I did and could read these poems and poets on some level, even as a child, and I profited enormously thereby as I grew older and explored more and more of the hidden places of meaning they contained. The important thing, though, was that, even on the twelve-year-old level, these great poems were accessible. Always bear in mind that to be accessible does not mean to be superficial—a fact that can be very reassuring.

2. Your poem should deal with a broadly-shared human experience.

It's a free country. You can write about whatever you want to write about. But if you want to publish the poems that you write, you should deal with broadly shared human experiences, and the more broadly shared the better.

Love is a broadly shared experience. Necrophilia is not.

Anxiety is a broadly shared experience. The details of your personal bankruptcy are not. And so on.

I think that most of us tend to recognize in ourselves and in others feelings, needs, compulsions that we all have in common, so this may be an easy requirement to satisfy. We simply have to be careful not to let the shared quality become submerged and hidden in the part of it that is personal to us alone.

Billie Varner is a North Carolina poet whose work I was instrumental in publishing. She writes about the simple relationships in her life, and she does so in a way that we can all immediately recognize as *our* experience, not simply the pains and pleasures of Billie Varner. Billie published her first book, *Come Share My World With Me,* when she was in her sixties. She later published two more volumes, all of which sold out their initial printing. In the fall of 1990, my company, Venture Press, published her *Collected Poems.*

Billie Varner is no academician. Purely literary devices and artifices are foreign to her. But she has wonderfully immediate access to her feelings and to the world around her. Her great success stems wholly from the fact that in her simple, lucid, and unpretentious verse she taps directly into the infinite well of shared human experience.

3. Your poem should treat a subject for which there is a market.

I can hear the mumblings now: "Poetry is above such mundane considerations," you may be saying. To which I reply, "Not for the poet who wants to be published, and published regularly."

Even the most highbrowed, allusion-prone academic poets write for a market. They write for journal editors who are on the lookout for others who share their abstract and literary view of life. They tend to experience life as strained through the sieve of the literary tradition, discarding all that doesn't seep through. Such a poet, intensely aware of the needs of the market he is aiming for, would not dream of sending a simple rhyme about, say, his daughter's first date into the rarefied editorial atmosphere of one of these journals. His submission would be rejected. The poetry might be good, but the subject matter would not be right for the periodical in question.

Some examples of marketable topics? Inspirational themes find a warm reception these days in many publications. There are scores of denominational magazines, newspapers, and newsletters hungry for such material, and their editors will be pleased to hear from you. These publications offer happy hunting grounds for the poet still trying to break into print. If the subject matter is right and the poem well-written to boot, then you stand a very good chance of getting a serious reading. Best of all, once you're in, repeat publication of other poems becomes a real possibility.

> The truth is that even the most high-browed, allusion-prone of the academic poets writes for a market. He writes for journal editors who are on the lookout for others who share their abstract and literary view of life.

I have said that I edited and published a regional magazine. This was *Tar Heel: The Magazine of North Carolina,* a slick paper, full color state magazine. Its editorial format leaned heavily toward lifestyle, historical-nostalgia, and tourism. I did not advertise that I would publish poetry, but whenever I received a sheaf of poems from a writer, I always read them with interest.

Some of these, I found, were very well written, but I couldn't use them. The subject matter was wrong. I needed poems about people, places, and events immediately recognizable to my readers. That is to say, the poems needed a bit of local color, and that local color had to be Carolinian, or at least compatible with North Carolina people and places. In style, the verse had to be accessible. Within those limits, I chose the very best of what was submitted to me, and I am happy to say that I was able to publish some very good work indeed. But first, the *subject matter* had to be right.

My magazine was not the only publication catering to this same readership. There was *The State* magazine and *We the People of North Carolina,* as well as assorted lesser ones. An enterprising poet could have seen that there was, indeed, a market for the kind of poetry I was accepting at *Tar Heel* and slanted his work toward it. The same pieces might also have been adapted for similar magazines in other states.

The poet, to be happily and consistently published, must analyze the markets, define the markets, and write poems with subject matter appropriate to them. Or, at the very least, after having written a poem, analyze the markets to see where to send it. My experience is that the first alternative is much more likely to bring success.

4. Your poetry should, whenever possible, be timely.

Publishable poetry is often timely poetry. This is true in a general and in a particular sense. In the general sense, publishable poems, if they are time-sensitive at all, relate to events, concerns, conflicts, or movements that many people share, and they are submitted at the time of this sharing.

Delay in submitting timely material can be fatal to publication possibilities. I once received a manuscript from a public school teacher who had been in Berkeley during the early days of the free speech, anti-war movement of the sixties. She had gone there from the small southern town where she had spent her entire life up to that time. The culture shock was enormous, and she told about it in an engaging, personal way.

Her work was good. At an earlier period—when it was still timely— I might have been tempted to publish it. However, by the time the author had pulled it out of her files and mailed it off to me some twenty-five years had passed. The themes were dated, the personal reactions and contradictions she described no longer vital for a new generation of readers. The material, as well-written as it was, was old hat.

In its most particular sense, timeliness leads to the production of occasional verse—poetry tied to a holiday or other special occasion. Christmas poems get published at Christmas, patriotic poems on the

Fourth of July, sweetheart poems on St. Valentine's Day. And they are published widely, in newspapers, magazines, newsletters, and every other possible kind of printed and readable product.

If you wish to submit occasional verse, do so several months in advance. Christmas poems should be sent out in late summer, Independence Day verse in January or February. You submit early because editorial decisions are made far in advance of publication. You want to allow yourself time to get your poem back in the case of a rejection and resubmit it elsewhere before it is too late.

5. Publishable poems are of manageable length.

Even those editors who love poetry and do whatever they can to support poets and publish their work face very real space problems. Publishing is a business. Space is expensive. Every item published must pay its way. When the editor of a magazine does find a poem that he likes and wants to publish, he must find a place for it. If the poem is too long he simply will not accept it, knowing that he will never have adequate space at his disposal.

How long is too long? I would say that a poem is unlikely to find a ready market in a general interest magazine if it runs longer that one-third of a magazine page. With poetry, the rule is that less is better. A one-sixth page poem will be even more easily published. Verse requiring two-thirds of a page or more is unlikely to find a home in the consumer magazine market.

In a sense, poetry is treated almost as filler. It is used when there is "leftover" space at the end of an article and no advertising has been sold to fill that space.

6. Publishable poems occupy a recogniziable niche.

You can gradually build a magazine market for your work when you become known for producing good verse of a particular kind or on a particular theme. This is especially true for poets who write humorous verse. An example would be the wordplay verses written by Willard Espy, which, for a while, were published monthly in *Writer's Digest*. Espy carved out a niche for himself. He built up a faithful following that editors could rely on.

Other specialties? Erma Bombeck has built a following for her prose observations on family life and relationships. Poems in the same humorous and insightful vein might build a reputation and find ready reception for anyone capable of writing them. Other themes will occur to you, growing out of your own experience. Once an editor accepts your work and finds that his readers like it, he will be open to other pieces of the same type. In this way an acceptance becomes the beginning of an ongoing relationship rather than a one-time stand.

7. Thematically related poems make publishable (and saleable) books.

I have a formula that has served me well in testing book ideas for success. It is this: *Books can be profitably published and sold when they appeal to a large number of readers in a limited geographical area.* When a publication meets these criteria, I know that I can sell it. There are many potential buyers, and they are concentrated in an area that I can cover without a national sales organization.

City magazines, city and county histories, and many other publications fall into this category, and the independent publisher who knows how to bring them out can make money thereby.

Poets can use the same criteria for testing ideas for books of verse. I recently published a book of poems by North Carolina poet Joseph Bathanti. It was work of the highest quality, with no concession whatsoever to the merely commercial. Just very good poems by a very good poet—a book that I was quite proud to publish.

Two things made me believe that I could sell enough of Bathanti's books to at least break even on the project. The first of these was the fact that the poems had all been written in and about the land and people of one North Carolina county. They were thematically related. I gave it a title that reflected this fact, and put a powerful, easily recognizable photograph of the county courthouse on the cover. I knew I would be able to sell quite a few copies of the book, *Anson County,* in the county itself. I also knew that all North Carolina libraries would be good prospects for buying a copy. As a matter of fact, the Anson County Development Commission, within a few weeks of publication, bought enough copies to defray over half of the out-of-pocket production costs. I think that *Outer Banks Poems*, or *Savannah in Verse*, or *Visions of Atlanta* would sell as well—at least well enough to recover costs and make a modest profit.

The related themes need not be geographical, although the marketing problems become more difficult when they are not.

The second reason I knew that I could afford to publish *Anson County*, by the way, was that I knew the poet to be a very good reader of his work, an active presenter. Few books of poetry are sold in bookstores. Most are sold at readings or at other special occasions where they can be sold and signed by the poet himself. Joe Bathanti, by virtue of his talent and energy, was a self-promoter. It was he who sold the first $1,000 dollars worth of books to the county development people.

8. The market-sensitive poet strives to create personal, public visibility. The poems that he writes thereby become more publishable.

It is not good enough to *be* a poet. If you want to get published, it also helps to be *known* as a poet. You will have to accept the fact that, when faced with a choice of merely good poetry by a better known author and great poetry by an unknown, the editor will too often go for the name recognition. It is a stronger choice for his magazine.

Among my friends are writers who, though no better and no worse than many others, always seem to be getting into print, especially in state and regional anthologies and collections, as well as in area literary publications, newspapers, and magazines. They are able to do this because they have created a public visibility for themselves, at least among the limited group of individuals who control these publications. They join writer's groups, apply for grants, give talks. They serve on editorial boards and arts council boards. Often they get themselves into the position of being one of those instrumental in awarding grants—a very strong position indeed.

They are everywhere, all the time, in the arts community of their region. Consequently, they get published when others don't. They give public readings and speeches at the drop of a hat. They organize "poets in the schools" programs, participate in writer's conferences, lead semi-

On Revision

Unless you're a closet Shakespeare, your words will never fall onto the paper just right on your first try. There are too many words in the language, too many shades of meaning, too many opportunities to be just a bit more precise or effective. Your first try can never be just retyped and shipped off to a waiting editor. Would-be writers who make that mistake become has-beens before they ever break into the field.

—Franklynn Peterson and Judi Kesselman-Turkel,
The Magazine Writer's Handbook

On the Art of Poetry

A poem is not only different, but means more than its prose paraphrase. It has physical shape (the black words as they lie on the white page): it has a musical configuration which, in itself, as sound, is expressive.

—Herbert Read, *The Forms of Things Unknown*

[A poem] is symbolic, and has the purpose of those symbolic talismans which medieval magicians made with complex colors and forms, and bade their patients ponder over daily, and guard with holy secrecy, for it entangles ... a part of the Divine Essence.

—William Butler Yeats

There is no royal road to good writing; and such paths as exist do not lead through neat critical gardens, various as they are, but through the jungles of self, the world and of craft.

—Jessamyn West

> It comes as a surprise to many poets to learn that few books of poetry are sold in bookstores. Most are sold at readings or at other special occasions where they can be sold and signed by the poet who wrote them.

nars, and talk to every group that will have them. Such poets are far more likely than others to have a *book* of their poems brought out. If publishing a book of your poetry is your ultimate goal, then developing this kind of public visibility is one major avenue to success.

There will be much more on this important topic in the chapter devoted to self promotion.

9. Finally, publishable poems are well-written poems.

No matter how much attention you pay to the marketing and purely commercial aspects of your work as a writer, the poems you submit must reflect your very best efforts at the poet's craft. There are very few—if any—new ideas, and probably no really new human experiences. What makes a poem is not so much *what* you talk about as *how* you talk about it.

A young writer once asked the great French poet Stéphane Mallarmé where he got ideas for his poems. "My dear fellow," Mallarmé replied, "you don't make poems with ideas. You make them with words." It is the writer's craft, the powerful play of words, rhythms, and images, that transforms a feeling or a thought into a poem.

Always keep at it until you get it right. Don't be satisfied with anything less than your best. Don't leave a kink in a line that you haven't taken time to smooth out. Don't satisfy yourself with the almost right image when you know the right one is lurking somewhere in the shadows of your mind. Always remember Mark Twain's marvelous admonition the for the writer. The difference, Twain said, between the almost right word and the right word is the difference between the lightning bug and the lightning.

The Great Wheel of Publishing

This writing and publishing circle must be closed, or the business of writing will not work.

Chapter Four / How to Get Published in Magazines

My years as editor of a regional magazine and a small book publishing company have taught me that the vast majority of queries and submissions of fiction, non-fiction, and poetry alike that arrive each morning on the editor's desk are so unprofessional in presentation and appearance as to start out with two—or even three—strikes against them. Many show wildly mistaken assessments of the editorial needs of the publication to which they were sent. The market research simply was not done. Too often these submissions were not timely, not accessible to the reader, not of the proper length....and so were simply not publishable.

These are sad observations, but they are all too true. Yet, correctly submitting your poems to magazines is a simple, straightforward process. There are just a few rules to follow on the positive side and some pitfalls to avoid on the negative. That's not so much to remember, but each item on the list is very important. Remember that you want the editor who evaluates your work to do so in the most favorable frame of mind possible. You may be new to the game. You may be totally inexperienced. You may be the rankest amateur. Fine. The important thing is not to look like one.

Step One: Research the Market

When you truly research possible markets for your poems, a strange thing happens. You become happily aware that there are far more outlets for your verse than you ever thought possible. If you are a careful writer and knowledgeable in your craft, the odds of finding a publisher are very much improved when you utilize the methods suggested in this chapter. With luck, you will gradually begin to see your work in print, at first from time to time, then more and more frequently.

How do you go prospecting for poetry-publishing periodicals? Here are some ways to get started:

- You can begin with a reference book like *Poet's Market*, published by Writer's Digest. You will find many consumer and small press magazines that publish poetry listed in this directory. Select those that seem most likely to be interested in *your* work. When you have exhausted this source, though, you will have done nothing more than scratch the surface. Scores of regional and specialized publications will not be listed there.
- Check Len Fulton's *Directory of Literary Magazines and Small Presses* (Dustbooks) for the names of literary publishers that may be interested in your work.
- Next, go to your local library and browse through the periodical shelves. Pay special attention to regional magazines and house magazines. I am thinking, for instance, of a magazine like *Carolina Country*, which goes out monthly to several hundred thousand members of the North Carolina Rural Electrification Cooperative. Most of us would never think of this magazine, yet, for the right poem of the right length on the right subject, it just might offer the opportunity you are looking for, even though it seldom publishes verse at all. A friend of mine recently wrote and illustrated a nifty little sixteen-page pamphlet that he titled *The Great Sweet Potato Cookbook*. The recipes in it were entirely in rhyme. *Carolina Country*, with its strong emphasis on home and garden, might have been perfect for these rhyming recipes. Placement there could easily have led to a continuing series (The Rhyming Gourmet) and even a book. Anyone writing this kind of verse for a magazine of such powerful circulation will certainly build a broad base of faithful readers and the kind of strong name recognition on which successful careers are built.
- Search, too, for magazines published by private industries and for trade magazines. Topical poems on subjects of special interest to the editors of these magazines could very well find a home in their pages. Use your imagination as you study the

offerings on the reading room shelf. Look for a slant, an approach, as you pick up each and every publication. Ask yourself, "How can I fit in here?" More often than you think, an idea will pop into your mind. As is the way with such ideas, some of them will be good ones and will work for you.

- Don't neglect the newspapers. In addition to the daily papers there are smaller tabloids of various kinds in many communities that cater to those interested in books, cultural events, and other arts. These may be just right for you.

- Consult the periodical directories, such as *Gebbie's All-in-One Media Directory* and the *Gale Directory of Publications and Broadcast Media.* These valuable reference books contain listings for all but the most obscure publications, listed by type of editorial content.

- When you find a magazine you think that you will want to submit to, write to request writer's guidelines. Don't forget to send an SASE along with your request. These guidelines will probably be prepared primarily for writers of non-fiction articles, but the general information they contain about subject matter, editorial requirements and the general slant of the magazine will be quite valuable to you. Look through the magazines in doctor's offices, dentist's waiting rooms, the seatbacks of airplanes, the reception areas of businesses that you may enter during the week. Be ever on the alert for possible outlets for your work. Carry a small notebook with you at all times to make note of the vital information (names, addresses) of magazines, newsletters, and other publications that you find in such places.

- When in doubt, go ahead and add a publication to your list. As you begin to submit in a systematic way, you will have ample opportunity to weed out the unsuitable names and add others that seem more likely to bring success. You are like a prospector looking for gold. You explore every possible source. Neglect one and you risk missing precisely the vein where the mother lode lies. Take careful notes on your market research. Much of what goes into our minds doesn't stick there.

The Professional Writer

You won't get far by . . . being timid and underestimating your abilities or worth. I meet students and new writers who say: "I'd write a story for nothing in order to get into print!" That, and any notion remotely akin to it, is the attitude of an amateur, and editors, though often willing to gamble on a new writer, are never drawn to amateurism. The professional writer is not one to stand around humbly, like a beggar at the back door. He tries to offer something good, and in a manner that suggests self-confidence and self-esteem.

—Hayes Jacobs

You can find the addresses of all consumer, newsstand, house, specialty and trade magazines in *Gebbie's All-In-One Media Directory.* Daily and weekly newspapers are listed, too. You can order your copy from www.Gebbie.com.

RECOMMENDED RESOURCE

Note the name of the publication, the address, the editor's name (if there are several editors, choose the one that seems most appropriate), a brief description of the needs of the magazine and its editorial policies. Make a note of the ways that you think your work can fit in with these policies. If you find any poems in the editions you look at, note the subject matter and *the average length.* Finally, make careful note of ideas for poems that occur to you in the course of your research and that you will write for the express purpose of filling a particular editorial need.

- Scour the internet. See the later chapter on internet resources for tips on how to do this effectively.
- When you have completed your basic market survey you should have scores—perhaps even hundreds—of names on your list. Some of these names will be known to very few poets, since most will not have done the spadework necessary to turn up the hot leads.

Create "Poem Packs"

With your prospect list in hand, you now study the poems that you have on hand and that are ready to make the rounds of the editorial offices that you have targeted.

Let's say that you have forty top-notch, publishable pieces ready to mail out. Study these poems with an eye to creating what I will call "poem packs." These will be made up of verses with compatible themes and of compatible lengths, thus appealing to similar markets. In addition, each poem included in the pack will have passed a significant number of the tests of publishability outlined in chapter 3. Since editors generally like to see more than one poem at a time, but grow restless at the prospect of reading more than four, I suggest that each of your poem packs contain at least two and no more than four pieces.

Now give each poem pack a number and carefully note the titles of the poems that it contains. You may eventually want to break them up into new combinations, and you want to know at a glance which editors have seen which of your poems.

The Key to Success: Organized Marketing

You have created these poem packs to facilitate your marketing effort and to help produce some early results. You are now ready to begin an intensive round of submissions, keeping all of your poems out for consideration all of the time. Since you have dozens of magazines on your prospect list, it doesn't make sense to send everything out serially, waiting to hear from one publication before sending a batch out to another.

You will make up a "submissions log" for each poem pack. I include one that works for me in this chapter. I attribute my first sale to a major magazine to the rigorous, unrelenting use of this simple form. It enabled me to keep my submission alive until someone bought it, and that someone (*Esquire* magazine) turned out to exceed my wildest expectation. Prior to adopting the self-imposed discipline of my submissions log, I allowed my queries to spend more time in my desk drawer than they did in the editorial offices of magazines. The same success can come to you, too, when you institute a campaign of intensive, organized marketing.

What we are talking about here is a well-planned effort whose goal is to get you published—as well and as often as possible. You simply can't keep up with the whirlwind activity of this method without this record-keeping. Neglect to use this form and you will forget what has been sent where. You will delay resubmitting poem packs that have been returned to you because you can't remember where you wanted to send them next.

Here's what you do:

- At the head of each form, fill in the number of the poem pack whose submissions it records.

- Then list, one after the other, the names and addresses of ten possible markets for these poems.
- Send the pack to the first name on the list.
- If your work is accepted, great! If not, send it out again, *within twenty-four hours of its return.* Make this a hard and fast rule. *Never* keep a poem pack on hand more than a day. You can't sell what people can't see.

Gradually, you'll begin to build a second, higher priority list, made up of the names of editors who either buy your work, express an interest in your work even though they don't buy, or include an encouraging, handwritten notation of some kind on their rejection slip. You will want to send something to those on this priority list at least once a month until you've got nothing more to send.

The Professional Submission

The submission itself is quite simple to prepare. Yet, simple as it is, not only some, but *most,* of the poets who have sent their work in to me over the years have failed to follow the basic rules of literary etiquette. The goal is to make your poems easy to handle, easy to read, and easy to think about. Here are the rules of he game:

- Each poem will be typed, double-spaced, on a sheet of good quality, 24 lb., white bond paper.
- In the upper left hand corner of the page bearing your poem, you will write your name and address.
- In the upper right hand corner, note the rights that you offer for sale. Most editors are quite content with the basic first serial rights offer.
- Many of your poems will be complete on one page. In the event that a poem requires two or more pages, be certain that the pages are numbered sequentially and that your name and the rights information appear on each page. Most word processing programs can handle this "header" information and save you the burden of having to retype it quite so often.

- Include a cover letter, personally addressed to the appropriate editor. (See "How to Read a Magazine" in chapter 5. If you don't know the editor's name, call the magazine and ask for it. Avoid a "Dear Editor" letter. Your one-page cover letter very succinctly (1) offers the poems for consideration; (2) gives some subtle (I emphasize *subtle)* indication that you are familiar with the editor's publication and its needs; and (3) briefly mentions your best credentials ("My poems have appeared in..."), if any. You should omit this section rather than list the time you had a quatrain appear in the high school newspaper or on your family Christmas card. This cover letter, like the poems themselves, is cleanly typed on good white bond.
- Include a self-addressed, stamped envelope.
- One last recommendation is a personal preference. I do it with my own work, even though it is a bit more expensive. I do not fold my submissions for mailing in a standard, number 10 envelope. I mail them flat in a large, white catalogue envelope. These unfolded submissions, even when just a few pages long, are easier to handle and easier to read. More than any other kind of writing, poems have a visual impact on the reader. It is good to see them entire, on a flat, unfolded piece of paper. However, this procedure is certainly optional, and I leave you to make up your own mind which is better for you.

Two key sources for market research, both edited by Len Fulton : *The Directory of Literary Magazines and Small Presses*, and *The Directory of Poetry Publishers*. Always check to make sure that you are using the latest edition.

RECOMMENDED RESOURCE

Beginner's Mistakes You Should Avoid

Newcomers to the ranks of professional writing reveal their inexperience in characteristic ways. Carefully avoiding these errors will put you in a much stronger marketing position.

Submissions Log: Poem Pack # 1		
Titles: Birdland Rhapsody, Staten Island Blues, Piano Man, Go!		
Where Submitted	**Date**	**Result**
Little Review	1/5/99	"Not right"
West Coast Poets	2/15/99	No, but wants to see more
New Yorker	3/4/99	Accepted "Staten Island Blues"

How to Read a Magazine

How to read a magazine? It's obvious, isn't it? You open it from the front or (as some do) from the back and leaf through, stopping to peruse items of interest to you. You do it that way, that is, unless you are a writer researching markets, in which case you go about it differently. The poet or prose writer who wishes to place a poem or an article in that magazine will look analytically at some items that casual readers normally avoid.

Masthead: The masthead appears within the first few pages, and lists editors: managing editors, senior editors, and plain, everyday editors. If you're lucky there may even be a poetry editor. The masthead will give you a specific name to address your query or submission to, an important item in your contact strategy.

Articles and Poems: You will look at articles and poems with an eye to determining typical subject matter, style, length. What kind of writing is featured? In a recent issue of *Atlantic Monthly*, I note six poems, one on the human consequences of the economic law of supply and demand and a clutch of five thematically related poems, labeled "More Marriages." The longest of these runs to 35 lines. The most immediately recognizable name is that of Donald Hall. The poems are very good. This is obviously not a break-in market.

Advertising: Analyze the advertising to determine the economic profile and lifestyle characteristics of readers whom the advertisers evidently wish to reach. Editors will be more interested in work that also interests this demographic group.

Media Kit: For a thorough understanding of a magazine, find the address of the advertising department in the masthead, and request a media kit. This will be full of demographic and circulation information, and will usually contain a sample magazine.

- Do not include a note telling how much your family and friends think of your talent and how they encouraged you to send these poems in.
- Do not inform the editor that you are sure that these poems are just what his readers have been waiting for and that you feel certain that they will love them. Leave such decisions up to the editor.
- Do not include notice of copyright on your poems. Under the terms of the current copyright act, your work is protected anyway. Notice of copyright on a submission suggests legal problems and hints that you may be difficult to deal with. Your editor may want to buy first serial rights, all rights, or no rights. Time enough to worry about copyright after the deal is done. However, this item is optional.
- Do not submit poems in longhand. No one will take time to decipher them.
- Don't specify what payment you want. This is for later. When an editor accepts your work, he will tell you what his rates are. At that time you can accept or reject them, or perhaps negotiate an adjustment. In poetry, it's a buyer's market.
- Do not include photos or drawings to illustrate your poems, no matter how perfect you think your child's, your spouse's, or your lover's effort is. Art is handled by a magazine's designers. Writer-furnished art is seldom required. If you have something that is truly outstanding, you might mention it in your cover letter. If the editor responds and asks to see it, you can send it along.
- Don't send your poems out without an SASE.
- Don't give an editor a deadline for replying. Write a follow-up letter if there is a long delay in giving you a decision. If there is still no response, send your poem pack out to the next name on the list.
- Don't submit your work on fancy, colored paper.
- Don't submit your work on paper of non-standard size. Stick to eight-and-a-half by eleven.
  - Don't send out soiled or shopworn material. It is too easy

these days to print out fresh copies on your word processor.

A simple marketing method for getting your poetry into magazines? Yes, it is. But put it into action in the service of your own work and I will virtually guarantee you that if your poetry has any merit at all, it will sooner or later find its way into print.

Chapter Five / Who Will Publish Your Book of Poetry?

When you have published a number of poems in magazines, your thoughts naturally turn to publication in book form. Can you find a publisher for a collection of your work? It is not easy, but it can be done.

You stand a chance of interesting a small publisher in your book if you have some or all of these five things going for you:

1. A collection of good poems sufficient to make a small book— say three dozen or more, depending on length. It is a plus if some of these have previously appeared in magazines, journals, or other periodicals, thus creating the beginning of a positive track record for you and your work.

2. A thematically-related collection of poems that will be more easily marketed and stand a decent chance of selling out a modest first collection. A young poet recently showed me some of her work, which I found to be written with great sensitivity and with a firm grasp of her craft. One of the poems was entitled "Key West Cats." Since the poet lived in South Florida, I told her I would publish a collection of her verse if she could put together three or four dozen poems on the same theme— the Keys and their more colorful denizens, human and feline alike. I had no doubt that I could sell the collection in the Keys at bookstores and gift shops and at least break even on the project, while still paying a modest royalty to the poet.

3. A willingness (which you clearly communicate to your publisher) to assume the responsibility for self-promotion and for publicizing and selling your book. Give details of what you plan. This is nowhere near as hard as it seems. A self-promotion starter kit is given below, and much more follows in later chap-

ters. These promotional ideas are easy to use and *they work.* Remember, if you want to be successful, it is not enough to *be* a poet. You have to see to it that potential readers *know* that you are a poet.

4. The desire, energy, and know-how to make it happen. You supply the poems, the desire and the energy. I supply the know-how.

5. A willingness to assume some or all of the out-of-pocket expenses for publishing your book, whether from a grant, institutional support (the college or school you work for, for instance) or your own bank account. As I have said many times in this book, it is not only permissible but usually *expected* that poets will participate in the expense of the publication of their work.

The Changing World of Publishing

Publishing today is a highly diversified enterprise. It is no longer centralized in the metropolitan areas of New York and Boston, though this was the case just a few years ago. The technological revolution known as desktop publishing, along with the development of very affordable short-run printing techniques, has made it possible for many small—even minuscule—publishing companies to rise and flourish at reasonably viable levels of activity all across the country.

As a result, there are likely to be more book publishers out there than you can possibly imagine. I recently attempted to contact and list every publishing company in my home state of North Carolina. I thought it would be an easy task, requiring a day or two of research. I was very, very mistaken. I knew the largest regional houses—firms like John F. Blair, the University of North Carolina Press, and Algonquin Books. But there were dozens of others—Briarpatch Press, Mud Puppy Press, Ventana Books, North Carolina Wesleyan Press, Scots Plaid Press, St. Andrews College Press, and many others, including my own Venture Press. I had published books and magazines in North Carolina for years and thought I knew my way around in the literary world, but I was now discovering small presses that I had never heard of before. After a month's work, I was still adding new names to my list almost daily. You will encounter much the same situation in your part of the country.

Many of these publishing companies are quite small and little known to the general public or even to writers. Few of them will be listed in directories such as *Writer's Market* or even *Literary Marketplace*. Yet they do exist, and one of them may very well be interested in publishing your book.

You will need names and addresses of these editor/publishers in order to approach them. How do you get the information you need? In several ways:

- Visit bookstores specializing in literary, small press books. You will usually find these in university towns and seldom elsewhere. Browse the poetry sections. Collect names and addresses of publishers from the title and copyright pages of books that interest you.
- Join your state or local poetry society and network with the other members.
- Join writer's clubs and writer's support groups on the local and state level, again networking with other members.
- Contact book review editors of newspapers in your state. They can often help. A telephone call will work best. Newspaper work is hectic, with daily deadlines. Editors will not usually have time to answer mailed-in queries.
- Check the catalogue in the library of your state university. At the University of North Carolina at Chapel Hill, for instance, there is a North Carolina Collection with its own curator. The collection tries hard to include a copy of every book published in North Carolina or written by North Carolinians.
- Your state will have such a collection, too. If the curator is a gregarious sort, he or she may be willing to talk to you personally, sharing whatever information they have. Rarely, however, will the curator have all the facts you need. You will need to search through the card catalogue. Today you can usually do this by computer, often from your own home, making your task much easier and far less time consuming. Again, note the names and addresses of authors and publishers.

Where Do Ideas Come From?

Where do ideas come from? They are all around us and in us, if we would just pay attention to them and harvest them. The mind—your mind, my mind—is constantly emitting ideas, images, entire lines, even. These are what the great French poet Paul Valéry used to call "vers donnés"—powerful, ready-made lines that simply spring into consciousness, seemingly from nowhere. Often these ideas and images represent the best that our creative minds are capable of. Keep a notebook with you at all times. Capture these random thoughts in your notebook. Like a spark caught up in tinder, they contain great potential creative heat. Thoughts that you do not capture are lost forever.

Capturing thoughts in this way is what I call "mind-harvesting," and for me it is essential.

Submitting Your Poems

Your marketing effort begins when you approach the prospective publisher. You will have researched the needs and character of the publisher before choosing which ones to send your work to.

You will make your publisher aware of any credentials and credits that you have accumulated. Just make sure that the credits you enumerate are solid ones. If you have never been published before your task is more difficult.

> What is known as success assumes nearly as many aliases as there are those who seek it. Like love, it can come to commoners as well as courtiers. Like virtue, it is its own reward. Like the Holy Grail, it seldom appears to those who don't pursue it.
> —Stephen Birmingham

You've got to come across to your publisher not only as talented and deserving, but as energetic and promotion-minded as well. Of course, there is always the case of the poet whose first effort is a stroke of pure genius. If you are one of these rare birds, congratulations! But even in this case, it is you, as poet, who have to take the initiative to see that your work is published. Nothing happens of and by itself. You've got to *make it happen*.

Anticipate the Publisher's Mind-Set

Though most publishers understand and accept the fact that no one is likely to make much money on a book of poems, the publisher will certainly want to avoid a loss. To reassure the publisher that his investment of time and money in your work is safe, you will want to furnish him with the following items, information, and assurances:

- The poems themselves, very neatly typed and prepared according to professional standards. Your submission will be crisp and clean, not smudged and dog-eared. There will be no strikeovers or handwritten corrections. To submit your poems in this way conveys to the editor the impression that he

45

holds in his hands the work of a professional, someone who can be relied on to meet commitments and follow through on promises. Not to do so will brand you as an amateur unwilling to take the time to see that his own work is carefully prepared and presented.

- If any of your poems have been published in magazines, journals or other periodicals, provide a neatly typed list of these credits on your fact sheet. Provide tear sheets of any reviews, profiles, or other write-ups that will help establish you as a poet with marketable public visibility.

- If you have published a book of poetry in the past that sold well (500 to 1000 copies in a reasonably short period of time), then the publisher whom you are now approaching should be made aware of that success. Such facts will make it easier for him to believe that the same thing can be done again. How did you promote the book? Who bought it? For how much? Give all the details.

- Tell the publisher how you propose to help market your book once it is published. Where will you have opportunities to do readings? How often? The fact is that books of poetry are seldom bought in bookstores. They are almost always bought at readings, lectures, school appearances, and similar events. The publisher knows that no amount of effort on his part will sell your book. It is the poet alone who can do this. Let him know—in as much detail as possible—that you are ready, willing and able to do your part.

- Make it clear that, if need be, you can help with the costs of publication. I keep coming back to this fact because it is important. It is not unusual today for publishers to ask poets to assist in footing the bill for publication. This request rests on solid economic grounds. Even if an edition of 300 sells out, the publisher, after paying royalties, costs of production, office overhead, and other associated costs, will not show a profit sufficient to pay for his time. You can call your expenditure a subsidy, an investment, or come up with any other label you wish. Whatever you call it, this kind of arrangement is perfectly acceptable today, so long as the publisher is one of reputation and not a mere vanity profiteer. (More on this later.)

Such financial arrangements are the rule rather than the exception in the publication of poetry. As the highly-respected poet and mentor, the late Judson Jerome, pointed out in his popular *Writer's Digest* column some years ago, a book of verse is published for the poet. It is not a part of the publisher's normal, income-producing work. Why should the poet, Jerome asked, *not* pay part—or even all—of the out-of-pocket costs?

Such an arrangement is often called "cooperative publishing," and, when honest and straightforward, it is a wholly acceptable one. To check the *bona fides* of any publisher with whom you are considering a co-op deal, check the other books or chapbooks the company has published. Are they well designed? Is the verse in them of a quality that you would not mind being associated with?

Be ready to do your part. "Cooperation in cooperative publishing is a two-way street," Judson Jerome observed. "To interest a small press in bringing out my work I know I have to demonstrate that I am willing to do my part. For one thing, I understand their financial situation. I know how hard it is to sell poetry, and I don't expect publishers to publish it at a loss. I let them know where I will be giving readings and lectures, and I take copies of our book to peddle as I go. Some poets working with small presses help with typesetting, collation, with the physical process of getting out their books. And they pitch in when it comes to selling them. Much of my professional life has gone to making myself into a name—minor league though that name may be. My poetry will never sell like Jimmy Stewart's, but people who see my books are likely to have some idea of who I am. That matters. If you are a recluse like Emily Dickinson was, your publishing history (if any) is likely to resemble hers: mostly posthumous."

Cooperative publishing can be a professional and thoroughly workable arrangement. Such a system has, indeed, been the norm for many years in the field of academic publishing. It is rare to get a book published by any but the most affluent university presses without coming up with a sizable contribution to the cost of publication. Sometimes the subsidies come in the form of grants from local, state, or national foundations or arts organizations. Sometimes the author's home university or college will provide the necessary funds. Sometimes it is the author himself who foots the bill.

Is this "vanity publishing?" Absolutely not. The so-called vanity presses of the "New York Publisher Seeks Books" variety will publish virtually anything that is submitted to them that they won't go to jail for. Their sole motive is the profit motive. To indulge it they charge the author an arm and a leg and deliver virtually nothing, save embarrassment at being associated with their usually soiled reputations. Reviewers, who know all this, will not usually take the trouble even to browse through a book that bears the imprint of the vanity presses on its title page. They will, however, read the books published by even the smallest independent publishers, especially those that have built a reputation for quality. With the small publishers you can be in exemplary company indeed. The presses we are talking about avoid the "vanity" label like the very plague. Their chief motive in publishing poetry is to publish good poetry. They just want to avoid a negative balance sheet and so stay in business.

Money may talk in some circles, but among the reputable presses it will not get you very far without poems of real merit. You could not buy your way on to the University of North Carolina Press list or the Louisiana State University Press list for any sum of money. Only the highest quality will get you there. Books are read carefully and fastidiously evaluated. Only those found to be worthy are accepted. Then and only then does the question of money arise—at which point the university presses and other independent publishers will sometimes explore the possibility of an author-generated help in meeting some (or even all) of the costs of publication.

Chapter Six / Publish It Yourself!

There far more good poets than there are presses to publish them. The number of small and independent publishers—though greater than you may imagine—is still very small when compared to the number of books submitted to them. There are undoubtedly poems of true excellence tucked away in desk drawers and attics all over America because their authors failed, not as poets, but as marketers of poems.

Mark Twain tells the story of an individual who, having gone to heaven, witnessed a celestial parade of the greatest poets in history. At the head of the file, just in front of Homer and Dante, marched a little shoemaker from the backwoods of Tennessee. He was the greatest of them all, Twain explained. He was unknown because he never managed to get published.

You need not let that happen to you. Today there is a sure way, once and for all, to end your own frustration at writing good poems that you can't get into print: publish and sell them yourself. This is easier to do than you may think, and—contrary to what some may think—is quite honorable. Publishing a book is not a mysterious process; it is just a new skill with a gentle learning curve. And when you have done it once, you can do it again and again.

If the selling and marketing part worries you, bear in mind that you would bear the main burden of selling your books, no matter who published them. The only books of poetry that are likely to be sold are those sold by the poet himself or herself at personal appearances and readings. Such events are as easy to arrange when you publish your book yourself as when someone else does it for you. Plus you have total control over the design of your book, and you get to keep *all* the money you make when you sell a copy.

Though no one is likely to get rich writing poetry, self-published authors of verse often recoup all their expenses and make a modest profit if they are willing to do the required marketing.

It's OK to Self-Publish

In case there's any lingering doubt in your mind concerning the legitimacy of self-publication, let me take a moment here to set the record straight. Writers and others who have not been following the truly revolutionary changes in the publishing industry in the last few years may not be aware of the way in which the landscape has changed.

Almost twenty years ago now, Bill Henderson, founder of Pushcart Press, self-published his *The Publish-It-Yourself Handbook: Literary Tradition and How-To.* This book was a rousing success and sold edition after edition nationwide. Sales of this one title were adequate to build Henderson's one-man enterprise into one of the great success stories in the independent publishing movement of recent years.

Henderson was a man before his time. When he wrote his *Handbook,* the technology that has now put self-publishing within easy reach for anyone who truly wishes to get into print had not been invented. So the how-to part of his book is somewhat dated. The "literary tradition" section, however, did a very great service for the whole independent publishing movement. Henderson pointed out that self-publication had a long and noble history. Walt Whitman, Carl Sandburg, Stephen Crane, Edgar Allen Poe, and dozens of the greatest names in our literature all self-published at one time or another.

> There are many different kinds of poetry. The poets that I like write about themselves. The trick is writing about yourself so that you're writing about the reader, too.
> —William Greenway, in *Poet's Market*

Far from being a back-door entry into the world of published poets, self-publication today is booming and is *very* respectable. As money becomes tighter and as major publishers focus more and more exclusively on the quest for blockbuster best sellers, it has become inescapably clear that for books with limited sales potential—as all books of verse clearly are—self-publication is not only an acceptable alternative but often the *only* alternative.

The writing of books, manuals, and guides for self-publishing writers has itself become a mini-industry within the publishing field. Judith

Appelbaum, a long-time pro in the New York publishing field, has a book on the market called *How to Get Happily Published.* Appelbaum's book is one of the best on the subject that I have ever read. It tells the fiction and non-fiction writer how to approach the larger commercial houses, outlines strategies for getting careful readings from thoughtful editors, and much more. A very generous portion of the book is devoted to the how-to of self-publication, and this section has been growing with each successive edition of the book. This New York pro has no hesitation in treating self-publication as a perfectly feasible and totally acceptable alternative for many writers.

If you believe in your book and want to see it in print, bring it out yourself, utilizing the methods and strategies that I will outline in the following sections. In this way you guarantee that your book will be published. It will no longer languish, unread, in your desk drawer. It will be out in the world, on its own, where it will stand alongside other books of its kind on its own merits.

Self-Publisher's Checklist

Is your book of poetry a good candidate for self-publication? To find out, study the following checklist. You should be able to answer "yes" (even a qualified yes will do) to most of these questions:

- Does your poetry meet at least one or two of the criteria for publishable poetry outlined in Chapter 2?
- Are you willing to make the necessary effort to follow the production and design guidelines specified in Chapter 10?
- Are you willing to study and implement the marketing techniques specified in Chapter 6?
- Are you willing to schedule and give readings of your verse?
- Are you willing to accept the fact that the best you can do financially is make a modest profit on direct sales of your book?
- Are you willing to open yourself to public criticism? If you are fortunate, your book will be reviewed. Only time will tell whether most of these reviews will be positive or negative. When you publish you enter the larger world of literature. Like all other writers, you will savor your successes and lick

the wounds of your defeats—and all of us have both of them.

OK, you passed the test? Now let's go on and see how it is done.

Name Your Publishing Company

You may be a self-publisher, but the operative word is still *publisher*. Open any book on your shelf and look at the title page. You will see the title, the author's name, and, at the bottom of the page, the name of the publishing company (the "imprint," as it is called).

Harper & Row, Simon & Schuster, Alfred A. Knopf. . . these are all imprints that you will find on title pages, as are hundreds of other publisher's names.

When your book comes out, you will want it to look, feel, and be just like the products of any other publishing company. You will have to choose a name for your own imprint. You can be whimsical, poetical, practical—whatever you like. But keep the following points in mind.

- Do not name your company after yourself. Your name will be on the title page as author. Don't double up as publishing company name too. "My Book of Poems" by Sue Smith, Sue Smith Press is just too much of a good thing. Choose something else. There are several good reasons for this. When you see how well your own book goes, you may want to branch out and publish the work of other poets. They would probably prefer to have the work appear over a neutral imprint rather than one promoting your own name. They will want, and probably deserve, to be the only poet whose name appears on the title page.
- If your work is regional in tone, you may want to choose a regional-sounding name: Copper Canyon, North Point, Tar River Press are some successful ones that come to mind. Such regional imprints will attract the attention of reviewers for regional newspapers and magazines. The regional name gives them an immediate reason to pick up and browse through your book. If they like it, perhaps they will write about it. After

all, being up-to-date on literary activity in their geographical area is part of their job.

- Whatever you do, don't choose a name that belittles your new-born publishing company. I don't think I would go for "Last Chance Press" or "Better Than Nothing Books," for instance. Yet you would be surprised just how many people do precisely that.

Eschew Self-Deprecation!—Now and Evermore

Many writers—modest souls that they are—play the game of self-deprecation for all that it is worth. They play it to the point of doing themselves and their reputations real damage. Or, if not damage, then very little good. I know, because I used to suffer from this affliction myself—and still do, to some extent, when I am not careful.

> The thrust of good art...has always been to reveal something of the truth of human beings, reveal that it is precisely the thing or things that lie beyond the web of deceptions and virtualities than everybody weaves about themselves.
>
> —*Andrei Codrescu*

So project your talent and confidence, not your uncertainty and fears. When your book comes out, you immediately become that *avis rara,* the published poet. Smile. Beam. Give interviews. Take yourself seriously. Remember that it is a given of human nature: people, in forming opinions about us, take their cues from us. If we take ourselves seriously, so will they. If we don't do so, then there's little chance that anyone else will, either.

You have put all of your talent, your heart and your soul into writing the poems that you have published. Why then, when asked to sign a book, would you be tempted to cast down your eyes and murmur, "Well, if you really want me to." Or why, when handing someone your book to look at, would you be tempted to say, "This is just a little book of my poems," hang your head submissively to the side, and smile uncertainly.

I don't know why, but I do know that many writers suffer from a self-effacement syndrome so serious as to rob themselves of all believability. Remember that for others, particularly for non-writers, you, as a published author, are almost a mythic figure. Play the part. Be what you are—a writer and a darn good one. Such demeanor sells books and, besides, it is a lot of fun. If you are like most of us, your ego can use a little admiration from time to time.

Set Up as a Business

Get all the normal accoutrements of business: business cards, letterhead, invoices, statements, etc. If you want people to do business with you, you will have to be businesslike about it. And don't forget that as self-publisher, you are a businessperson. There will be significant financial benefits to you. Tax savings can be substantial. Your printing expenses, marketing expenses, travel on behalf of your book or in search of ideas, telephone, word processor or computer, dues and subscriptions, travel to writer's and publisher's meetings and conventions, and home office expense are tax deductible. If you are incorporated you, as president of your corporation, may be eligible for goodies like before-tax medical and life insurance. Check with your accountant.

Establish a Marketing Program

Set up a formal marketing program to bring your book to the attention of the public. Study carefully the chapters "The Unabashed Poet's Guide to Self-Marketing," "How to Give an Autograph Party," and "How to Give the World's Best Poetry Readings." Make a list of how you are going to accomplish all the things discussed in them. Schedule the implementation of this program in great detail. Make check lists to prod your memory. Do *what* you schedule yourself to do *when* you schedule yourself to do it. There will be a lot to do. Without these lists and schedules you won't get it all done.

Is it important that you do so? Decidedly so, since *in the business of selling books, nothing happens without marketing.* All this holds true whether you self-publish your book or whether someone else publishes it for you. As a published poet who wants to sell books, you have no choice: you are your own marketing department.

On Self-Publishing

Shall not each individual have the right to attempt, weak or strong as the attempt will be in proportion to the particular gifts involved, to give his work the kind of definition that is bestowed by presentation in a book? Time and the world will prove the book's value, for I am convinced that in mysterious ways, intangible forces sift the good from the bad, and the worthy will become known. In years to come, if the work merits a place in mankind's artistic heritage, what will it matter who published it? How unworthy are those "friends" who, impressed with name publishers, demean a self-published work in spite of its inherent merit.

Poet friends and even I often tried to disguise the fact that we were publishing our own work, because of the onus of the label self-published. We fabricated names of nonexistent presses, or I was asked to lend the name of my press to a friend's book to hide the fact that it was self-published. In time, I came to realize the folly and false vanity of such acts and to recognize the merit of such publication and the joy involved. Now I proudly list my own books under the title of my own press, Folder Editions, which has achieved a reputation among collectors and libraries for fine poetry books.

If the goal of the self-publishing poet is financial gain, he is living in a world of illusion. Since comparatively few people possess the ability to read good poetry with pleasure and understanding, the poetry field never has been and never will be a lucrative one. Joy in the work and a sense of creative achievement should reign. If sheer unrestrained ambition to see oneself in print is the motivation, then one should think twice before adding to the mountains of dead written matter which clutter homes and libraries. The question must be asked, "Will my work, in even a small way, enrich lives?

—Daisy Aldan, *Poetry & A One-Woman Press*

Poet Power

If all of this marketing and business talk seems crassly commercial to you or beneath your dignity as a poet, you are wrong. Your judgment springs from a self-defeating naiveté. Even the finest writers actively market their books and blow their own horns. Do you think that Dylan Thomas really enjoyed traveling around from campus to campus reading his poems night after night? Do you think that writers actually take great pleasure in small town TV interviews and bad hotels on coast-to-coast tours? Not really. There is, of course, a flush of pleasure during the first heady days and weeks. After that, public appearances—with notable exceptions—become a job to be done. Writers do these things because they know that they must do them to make their books sell.

Chapter Seven / The Anatomy of a Book: How to Design, Typeset, and Print Your Book or Chapbook

In the last chapter we went over some of the basics for setting up your own publishing company. In this one you will go step-by-step through the process of publishing your own book. You will learn:

- How to finalize your editorial design.
- How to get an ISBN number and list your book in national databases such as *Books In Print*.
- The elements of page and cover design.
- How a professional-looking book is structured.
- How to lay out a page.
- How to choose a suitable typeface and specify its size.
- The basics of front and back cover design.
- How to get your book typeset and made ready for printing.
- How to get your book printed at a price you can afford to pay. Your goal is to make a book that is both attractive and inexpensive to produce. You want it to look as good as or better than any other book, but you don't want to mortgage the farm to get it done.

In the discussion that follows I will refer you to some other books that focus exclusively on the production process, so that when you need additional information you will know where to find it. I find these books fun to read, and often dig out valuable nuggets of information from them. Those that I recommend are, in my opinion, the cream of the crop.

Still, your mind will be full of questions. How do you start? What do you do first? Second? After that? How much will it cost? What will the

The Art of Poetry

A poem not only is different, but means more, than its prose paraphrase. It has a physical shape (the black words as they lie on the white page); it has a musical configuration which in itself, as sound, is expressive.

—Herbert Read, in
The Forms of Things Unknown.

Always the seer is a sayer.

—Ralph Waldo Emerson, in
The Divinity School Address

Before people complain about the obscurity of modern poetry, they should first examine their consciences and ask themselves with how many people and on how many occasions they have genuinely and profoundly shared some experience with another....

—W.H. Auden

book look like? Who will print it? I know this because I had the same questions when I set out to bring out my own first self-published book.

Fortunately, I learned, the publishing process is not difficult. It's just different from anything you may have undertaken before. If you take it one step at a time, it is really quite easy. You can, too, so long as you will take it one step at a time and learn as you go. And while the first book you self-publish may require a bit of thought, preparation and even nervous sweat about the brow, those that follow will be a snap. Your hard-won knowledge will be very valuable to you throughout your career and well worth every ounce of the effort required.

Understanding the Language of Printing and Publishing

Like any other field, the book publishing and printing business has its specialized terms and its jargon. Throughout this chapter I have used certain terms that you may not be familiar with: *casebound, perfect bound, saddle-stitched, stock,* and many others. When confronted with a term you don't understand, simply ask, "What does that mean?" Printers are kindly folk. They'll be glad to tell you. Otherwise consult the *Pocket Pal* I recommended in an earlier chapter or the glossary of printing and publishing terms in the back of this book.

Deciding How Your Book Will Look

There is general agreement about what a well-designed and printed book should look like. Yours must look that way, too. This is not to say that there are not a great many possibilities for variation. Your book could be triangle-shaped with wildflowers drawn in the margins. It could be printed backwards. Every word in it could be printed in a different type style and size. Yes, you can do all of these things, but if you do them (and many self-publishers do these and other things just as unusual and self-defeating) you will create a serious and unnecessary handicap for yourself.

Remember that your poetry is the star of the show, and that the book that contains it should put nothing whatsoever between the reader and the direct enjoyment of your verse. Well-written poetry does not need decoration: it is its own decoration.

Your book *must look like it is supposed to look.* It must be cleanly designed and easy to read. Each poem should stand out like a gemstone set atop a simple platinum setting. The platinum is there simply to enhance the natural qualities of the stone and to hold it on the finger so that it can be admired by all who see it.

Some of the conventions of book design grow directly out of long use: it has been discovered and generally agreed over the years that certain page layouts and typefaces enhance communication. These patterns have been adopted as acceptable elements of design. Other elements, such as page size and binding, are based on physical necessities: the way presses work and the way a printed sheet of paper is folded.

We will take these one at a time in the pages that follow. For the moment, let me point out here that there are two ways that you can proceed from this point on. You can do most of the pre-press work (everything that must be done before the printer makes the prints for printing) yourself on your own computer. There are page layout programs like Pagemaker and QuarkXPress that will do a beautiful job for you, but which may be time-consuming to learn if you have never used them before. Other programs are simpler, such as Microsoft Publisher. Whatever program you use, I recommend that you design and typeset your book yourself. It may be a bit dicey at first, but the long-range benefits of what you will learn are considerable.

Trial and error will teach you most of what you need to know, will leave you in control of the layout of your book, and save you considerable money on typography. But, if saving a few hundred (or even a thousand or more) dollars is not a major concern for you, you may decide to have your printer or someone else typeset your book for you. However, since you will undoubtedly have more than one book to bring out over the course of your writing life, the time and effort you put into learning to design your own pages will be well spent indeed.

The Easy Way: Find a Model and Follow It

A tried and true technique for the person with no experience in book layout and design is simply this: find a book whose appearance pleases you and analyze it. Then make your own book look like the one you have chosen as a model. I used this method quite successfully when

I was a beginner in the publishing field. It's a little like learning to cook. As an amateur chef, I looked up recipes for the dishes I wanted to prepare and followed each step carefully. As time went on I began to play around with the recipes. Today, I almost never consult them. I have learned the powers and potencies of the various spices and culinary techniques and I combine them at will. I do the same thing now with book design, except that the possible variations are far more limited in publishing than they are in the kitchen.

 The *Pocket Pal*, published by the International Paper Company, is an excellent, concise guide to printing and production procedures and terms. See the "Resources" section at the end of the book for ordering instructions.

RECOMMENDED RESOURCE!

Shallow Pockets? Great! Make a Virtue of Necessity

If your pocketbook is skinny, make a virtue out of necessity. It is possible to design a barebones book that is nevertheless quite handsome. I have done it many times. I did it at first because of limited funds, but, even when I was not so strapped for cash, I continued to prefer the simple, more direct approach to design.

One warning: You should not harbor any illusions about making a big profit on your book. I often tell this fact of life to authors that I work with and just as often they don't believe me. They say they do, but they don't. Deep down inside they think they'll make a million.

Well, let me tell you it's just not likely to happen. Even when you sell out your entire first printing, the money comes in so slowly and in such relatively small quantities that it does not feel like profit or spend like profit, even if it *is* profit. Poetry is published for the love of poetry. If you will follow the marketing guidelines given in this book, you will make enough to cover your expenses, but you are not likely to do much more than that from the direct sale of your books.

However, there are many ways to profit from publication, and what you don't make in direct profits is often more than compensated for in

On Publishing Chapbooks

You can always publish chapbooks yourself. There is a long and honorable tradition of books privately printed, and not only by unknown writers—Jane Austen, Robert Louis Stevenson, Virginia and Leonard Woolf, and Robert Graves and Laura Riding instantly come to mind for their presses, not to mention William Blake, who did all of his own engraving and much of his own printing. Consider the beginnings of presses like New Directions or City Lights, Graywolf or Story Line: publisher and author were one and the same, or, if they weren't, the publisher and writers were friends. New waves in literature often get their start in vanity publications, because it is the only start they can get. It is instructive in this context to note that Ferlinghetti got his certification from Laughlin, and Laughlin from Ferlinghetti. Each of them, poor or rich, was once an unknown rebel who later became a preeminent arbiter, a paradigm himself.

—Richard Dey
Poets and Writers Magazine, December, 1998

other, far more varied ways. You can expect that the fringe benefits—personal and professional recognition, salary increases for teachers, income from workshops and seminars—will be more lucrative, depending on the energy and skill with which you take advantage of them.

Step-by-Step through Book Design and Printing

When you design your book you will be making a series of decisions, each of which affects all of the others. Don't get overwhelmed, just take them one at a time. When you finish, you will have sketched out the complete editorial and physical format of your book. Note how the designers of the published books have handled these matters and decide which you like best.

You can also consult a technical manual like Stanley Rice's *Book Design*, published by the R.R. Bowker company in 1978. You may have to get hold of this book through interlibrary loan at your local library. Another book that I strongly recommend—and this one ought to be on the reference shelf of every writer—is the *Chicago Manual of Style*, available at most well-stocked bookstores and through on-line booksellers such as Amazon.com. Look particularly at the first section, "The Parts of a Book."

Step 1: Choose Your Poems

The first step is a pleasant one: looking through your work to choose the poems that you wish to include in your book. If you have enough to fill 48 or more pages, you can produce a perfect-bound (see glossary) book. With fewer pages, you will have a saddle-stitched (glossary, again) chapbook. If you can put together a collection of poems that has a theme and an identity of its own, so much the better. If this theme can be tied to a place, and that place has many potential readers, you would be wise to utilize it. Remember the earlier discussion of collections like *Key West Cats* and *Anson County*.

Choose your best things. Resist the temptation to include everything you have ever written. Listen to your own mind and heart. Trust your instincts. They will tell you which are the strongest poems that you have written.

Step 2: Name Your Book

Next, give your book a name. Once you do, it will take on a reality, a kind of real-world density, that it has not had before. The choice of a title is an important one. The first step in selling a book is to get readers to pick it up and leaf through it. If they like what they see, they may read and buy. But you've got to get the book into their hands before anything else can happen. This is the job of the title. Here are some things to consider:

- Many books of poems utilize the title of the lead poem or the strongest poem in the collection as the title. Thus one often sees titles such as *The Waste Land and Other Poems* (T. S. Eliot) or *Howl and Other Poems* (Allen Ginsburg).
- I have found that linking the title to a place (especially a tourist destination) can be an effective selling tool: *Voices of the Outer Banks*, and, again, *Key West Cats* (combining animal lovers, island lovers, and the tourist trade in one strong package).
- Linking the title to favorite activities or sports can give you a boost toward the kind of sales you would like: *Sailing the Gulf Stream and Other Blue Water Poems*.
- If the theme and the tone of your poems are suitable, link them through the title to sentimental times and experiences. Think of the tremendous success of the self-published book, *When I Am an Old Woman, I Shall Wear Purple*. Maybe your book is susceptible to that kind of spin.
- Ride the trends: "Cowboy poetry," for instance, is currently enjoying a vogue, so a book called *Cowboy Songs and Sagebrush Ballads* would have a ready, well-targeted readership. Be alert for others that you can link your work to.

Find the hot spot of your own poems and come up with something irresistible. And, above all, come up with something you yourself like and are pleased with.

Step 3: Determine Page Size (Technically, "Trim Size")

What size will your pages be? Five-and-a-half by eight-and-a-half is

Emmanuel Haldeman-Julius, legendary creator of the "Little Blue Book" series, has a classic chapter on the importance of titles in his book, *The First Hundred Million*. It's as good as anything ever written on the subject. If you can't find a copy on your own, go to my web site at www.PubMart.com to download an ebook version.

RECOMMENDED RESOURCE

the most flexible and generally affordable page size, although six by nine runs a close second. The smaller of these is the size of a once-folded piece of cut paper, the kind that you buy in reams for copy machines and for typing. That page size enables you to fold up and stitch (staple) together your book yourself. Do not choose any non-standard page size. Such a choice may present production difficulties and will surely cost you money.

Step 4: Choose Your Stock (Paper)

The work "stock" is used by printers to refer to the paper your book is printed on. Normally, printers can match any stock samples you show them. They all have available sample booklets of various stocks that you can look through and choose among. If you are dealing with an out-of-town printer, which may very well be the case, ask them to send you samples of the papers that they use most frequently. Avoid fancy or unusual papers.

If you are printing two or three hundred copies of a short book (48 or fewer pages), then the cost of paper is secondary. However, special order paper always costs much more. Ask your printer to see samples of "house stock," that is, paper that he buys in large quantities and keeps on hand. These papers will always be far more affordable. If you are printing a longer run—say, 500 or 1,000 or more copies—or a book with considerably more pages, then your choice of stock will affect the cost of production to a far greater degree. You will want to look closely at it.

Step 5: Select a Typeface, Type Size, etc.

The actual work of putting the words on the page in their final, ready-to-print form is called typography or typesetting. Following is a list of the choices you will have to make, along with accepted guidelines for the use of type in books.

- *Choose a typeface.* There are a great many styles of type available. You will want to choose a very straightforward one that is easy to read. Avoid like the plague any fancy, "old English," script (cursive), or other specialty types. The use of these type styles in a book is the sign of the amateur. The main thing wrong with them is that they are hard to read. Remember at every stage of developing your book that your poems themselves are the most important thing. Do nothing to hinder access to them. Your word-processing or page layout program will have a selection of typefaces available, and you can experiment with these. If you decide to hire out the typesetting, ask the individual or company that is going to do the work for you to give you a type specimen sheet with the available type styles (called "fonts") shown on it. Choose the one that you find most readable.

- *Serif and sans serif.* There are two basic type styles: serif and sans serif. It is generally agreed that serif styles are more appropriate for the body of the poem itself, while the sans serif styles can be used, if you wish to do so, for titles. A serif typeface has the little curlicues on the tips of the letters and in the corners, such as where the top bar is connected to the stem of the letter "t." The text you are now reading is typeset in a serif style called Garamond. This sentence, on the other hand, is printed in a typeface called Helvetica, a sans serif (without serif) typeface. As you can see, the sans serif face is cleaner, but less interesting. Until you develop some expertise in using type, my advice is to stick to the serif faces for your poems, using sans serif faces sparingly, for titles and headings only.

- *Type families.* Typefaces come in "families." For each type style there is a roman version (referred to by many word processing programs as "regular"), an italic version, a bold roman version and a bold italic version. As an example, here is the complete Garamond family, in which the text of this book is set:

This is Garamond roman
This is Garamond italic
This is Garamond roman bold
This is Garamond italic bold

It is best to use no more than two type families in the same publication, preferably one serif and one sans-serif.

- *Which typeface (family) to choose.* Typefaces have long and fascinating histories, starting with Gutenberg's first movable type in the late fourteenth century. Aficionados of typography know these histories and choose typefaces with the fastidious discrimination of the artist. However, it is not necessary to know all of this, although you could have fun learning about it. Most word processing and page layout programs come with a basic selection of very serviceable typefaces. If you follow my advice and do the typographic page layout yourself on your desktop computer, you will choose one of these. Which should you use? Simply print out samples of your poems in various type faces and choose the one you like best.
- *The size of the type and the "leading."* You will also be choosing some other aspects of type style. For instance, how big is the type? Type is measured in "points." There are 72 points in an inch. For a book of verse, I would recommend type no smaller than 10 points and no larger than 12. The space between the lines is called "leading" (rhymes with "bedding"), and is usually specified at least two points greater than the size of the type style. Thus, you might specify 10 point Garamond, with 12 point leading. Again, print out samples to

There are many ways to profit from publication, and what you don't make in direct profits is often more than compensated for in other, far more varied ways.

The Art of Poetry

The familiar contention that science is inimical to poetry is no more tenable than the kindred notion that theology has been proverbially hostile—with the Commedia of Dante to prove the contrary. That "truth" which science pursues is radically different from the metaphorical, extra-logical "truth" of the poet. When Blake wrote that "a tear is an intellectual thing/And a sigh is the sword of an Angel King"—he was not in any logical conflict with the principles of the Newtonian Universe. Similarly, poetic prophecy in the case of the seer has nothing to do with factual prediction or with futurity. It is a peculiar type of perception, capable of apprehending some absolute and timeless concept of the imagination with astounding clarity and conviction.

—Hart Crane

see which point size and leading looks best to you. If you are using an outside typographer, ask to have a single poem set in two or three sizes, then choose the one that you like best.

- *The text and the title of the poem.* A safe format, and one that I recommend, is to set the title in italic type, perhaps even bold italic, and in a size two points larger that the one you have chosen for the text. The title may also be in a sans serif face, to contrast with the serif face of the poem itself. There will be an extra line of space between title and poem. Titles and poems will be set "flush left," or, as the word processing and page layout programs may say, "left aligned." See the sample layout included with this chapter.

Step 6. Design the Page

In matters of page design, remember this basic rule: simple and symmetrical is always better. Overwrought and highly decorated pages smack of amateur design and will reflect badly on your poetry. You want the reader's entire attention to be focused on the verse. Here's what you do…

- *Decide how wide your margins will be.* How much space will you allow for left, right, top, and bottom margins of your pages? In a novel, where space is at a premium and the appearance of the words on the page, though still important, is less critical than in poetry, margins may be as narrow as one-half inch all around. In a book of poetry, wider margins work better. I would suggest one inch top, right, and left, and one and a quarter inch on the bottom, to allow room for the page number.
- *Position the page number.* The usual place for the page number is at the center of the page, just below the bottom margin line. It can, of course, be placed elsewhere. It can go on the bottom of the page or on the outside margin, but I personally don't think this looks as good in a book of verse. It can be placed at the top of the page, but in my view this distracts from the title of the poem, which is the most important element. If you do decide to put your page number at the top of

Examples: Flush Left, Centered, and Run Over

Back and Sides
Back and Sides go bare, go bare
Both hands and feet go cold
But God give me good ale enough
To keep my belly warm.

Top, left:

This poem is set flush left. The title is italic and the text roman (regular). The text is 11 points. Leading is 15 points. The title is 13 points.

Back and Sides
Back and Sides go bare, go bare
Both hands and feet go cold
But God give me good ale enough
To keep my belly warm.

Bottom, left:

The same poem with centered lines.

The selection below, from Song of Myself, *contains three run-over lines, "hands," "any more than he," and "hopeful green stuff woven."*

A child said,*What is the grass?* fetching it to me with full
    hands.
How could I answer the child? I do not know what it is
    any more than he.
I guess it must be the flag of my disposition, out of the
    hopeful green stuff woven.

the page, then the top margin must be widened accordingly.

- *Position the poem itself on the page.* Consistency and respect for the poem itself are the keys. The reader should not be surprised by a different design each time he turns a page.

- Each poem deserves its own page. Just as you would not squeeze two paintings or prints into a single frame, so let each of your poems have the surrounding page to show it off properly. The white space around the poem frames it for reading and contemplation.

- An exception to this rule may be made for very short pieces—haiku, for instance—but even here I prefer to enjoy each one in its own space.

- Place the poem on the page, beginning with the title in the upper left-hand corner of the type page area, with the text directly below. Both text and poem are aligned along the left page margin.

- If the poem is too long for a single page, choose a logical point for ending the text on one page and continue the poem on the next page. Try to lay out your book so that poems which run to two or more pages begin on a right hand page. Although this is not an absolute rule, it is desirable.

- Do not place a shorter poem on the bottom of a page which begins with the last stanzas of another, longer poem.

- When one line in a poem is too long for the width of the page, carry the remainder to the next space below, beginning about one-quarter of the way across the page. Treat all overflow lines in the same way.

- No matter how you decide to format your poem, the eye is the final judge. Print out, look carefully, and alter what you see to suit you.

Step 7. Put Your Pages Together in Sequence

The next step is to arrange your poems in the most desirable sequence. While doing this you will take into consideration such things as:

- The best logical sequence of subject matter or of form. All sonnets could run consecutively, for instance, or all haiku. But the choice is strictly up to you.

- Remember that, whenever possible, you want all poems more than one page long to begin on a right hand page and end on a left hand page.

Step 8. Prepare Front Matter

Open any book on your shelf. You will note that it includes a number of pages before the text actually begins. These pages constitute the "front matter" of the book, and they follow one another in a precise sequence. Every book will not contain every item on this list, but the sequence remains the same. Front matter pages include the following:

- *Half Title.* You may or may not have a half title. Such pages include only the title of the book. The half title is the first printed page the reader comes to. When you turn past the half title you find the full title page before you. The half title is merely a device for utilizing an extra page which may be there because of the way your book is laid out. The half title page is always optional. No one will miss it if it is not there.
- *Title page.* The title page has three elements.
    a. At the top of the page is the title of your book.
    b. A little further down is your name as author.
    c. And at the bottom of the page is the name of the publisher. Since you are publishing your own book, this will be the name that you have chosen for your publishing company. In the language of the publishing business, the publisher's name is referred to as the "imprint."
- *Copyright page.* The back ("verso") of the title page is the copyright page. This is something of a misnomer, since the page includes more than the notice of copyright itself.
    a. At the top of the page you may place a list of your other books or publication credits, titled *Other Books by...*, or *Other Poems by....*
    b. Next is your Library of Congress catalog number. The

form that you will need in order to obtain this number can be gotten from the Library of Congress web site.

c. Below this is the ISBN (International Standard Book Number) for your book. The ISBN is discussed elsewhere.

d. The ISBN is followed immediately by the notice of copyright, which is traditionally written as follows:

Copyright© 1999
by (Your Full Name)

e. The name and address of your publishing company may also be placed on this page if you wish, immediately before the notice of copyright.

f. *Acknowledgments page*. This is the place where you acknowledge permissions to quote and the previous publication of poems. Personal acknowledgments may also go here, but if there is a preface, they should be placed at the end of that section.

g. *Dedication page*. The dedication page comes next. The dedication is usually set in the same typeface as the text. It may be in italic type if the text is roman, or in roman if the main text is set in italic. The words "Dedicated to" are not necessary. The dedication may be centered in the middle of the page, or set flush right (aligned right) on the right hand side of the page.

h. *Epigraph page*. You may wish to place a short quotation from another writer or poet at the head of your book. This quotation is called an "epigraph," and it follows the dedication page. Here is an example of the use of an epigraph from one of my own books, a biographical study of Stéphane Mallarmé. On the epigraph page I quoted another French poet, St. Jean Perse:

When mythologies crumble,
the divine takes refuge in poetry.

Sequence of Front Matter Pages

1. Half Title
2. (Blank)
3. Title
4. Copyright
5. Acknowledgments
6. (Blank)
7. Dedication
8. (Blank)
9. Epigraph
10. (Blank)
11. Table of Contents
12. (Blank page, if necessary. Foreword must begin on a right-hand page)
13. Foreword
14. (Blank page, if necessary. Preface must begin on a right-hand page)
15. Preface
16. (Blank page, if necessary. Text must begin on a right-hand page)

I used this quotation because I felt that it set the tone perfectly for my study, which was called *Mallarmé and the Language of Mysticism* (published by the University of Georgia Press). If you have such a favorite quotation, place it on the epigraph page.

i. *Table of Contents.* List here each poem and the number of the page on which it begins.

j. *Foreword.* The foreword generally consists of a few paragraphs or pages about you and your book written by someone else. A foreword is used to lend credibility to a text. If you are a little-known poet, just starting out on your career, it would be quite advantageous to have a foreword written by a more widely-read poet or by a literary commentator or critic with instant name recognition.

k. *Preface.* In the preface, the author gives something of the background of his work (i.e., "I began these poems living in a small town in southern Mexico. The first poems, etc. . . ."). This general statement is followed by acknowledgments of contributions made by others to your work, if you wish to make any. Persons acknowledged may range all the way from those who inspired you to the faithful editor-proofreader-typist who helped you whip the manuscript into shape. The preface usually ends with the author's name and, perhaps, the place and year of writing. (The Chicago Manual of Style prefers no place and date, but places and dates nonetheless frequently appear.) If there were a preface to this book, it would close as follows:

—*Tom Williams, Fort Lauderdale, 1998*

Step 9. Calculate the Number of Pages in Your Book

Most books of poetry are fairly short. Forty-eight or 64 pages is a common length, with shorter chapbooks of 32 pages or even fewer not uncommon. Your book will simply be long enough to contain the best poems that you have and that you want to publish.

Bear in mind, though, that because of the technical requirements of printing and the way paper is folded to make a book, you will have to decide on a length that is a multiple of four, eight, or sixteen. Books that are going to be produced by quick printers are done in multiples of four, as are pages that you yourself will produce on a copy machine or run out on a laser printer. A good question to ask your printer is this one: "What is the most cost-effective length for this book?" You may find that because of the way the paper folds, it is just as cheap to print a 64 page book as a 56 pager. Indeed, I have seen cases where a 56 page book cost more than one of 64 pages.

Step 10. Design the Front Cover and Back Cover

I can't stress enough the importance of a good, strong cover. This need not be elaborate and expensive; it is better if it is not. But it should be clean and professional in appearance. Avoid at all costs any amateur art on your cover. Poets who consult me on their publication projects often suggest that this or that "nice" drawing by themselves or by some relative be used as a cover. I have never, ever seen one of these drawings that was good enough to do the job. So I would suggest a general rule: no drawings on the cover by family or friends. Here are some acceptable ways to approach cover design:

- *You can use type alone.* Effective covers can be designed using type alone. Some examples of these are included within this chapter.
- *You can use clip art.* You may find old wood cuts or other art in the public domain within the "clip art" collections of most major bookstores.
- *You can use a photograph.* A black and white photograph is inexpensive to use. If you have one related to your theme, it can work well for you. See the *Anson County* cover sample on page 80.
- *You can use symmetry.* As with the interior of the book, strive for a simple, direct, symmetrical cover design. Symmetry is a great refuge and invaluable partner for the inexperienced designer.

On the back cover, put the following elements:

- At top of the back cover, put one single line to create interest in the book: "A New Collection of Poems from the Winner of the National Poets Award," for instance.
- A few descriptive sentences about the collection.
- A picture of the poet (good picture, preferably informal. Not a mere mug shot) and two or three paragraphs about the poet.
- In the lower left hand corner, put the ISBN and the price.
- In the lower right hand corner, put the bar code. Make it approximately one inch high. Most bookstores now require bar codes on books that they sell.

Step 11. Decide How Much Color to Use

Use no color other than black in the interior of your book. On the front and back covers, you can use two colors (black counts as a color) without incurring too much extra cost. However a full color photograph will add several hundred dollars to the cost of printing. With imagination, a fine cover can be designed in black ink alone. I have done this many times.

Step 12. Decide How to Bind Your Book

There are two basic choices when it comes to deciding what kind of binding you want to give your book: paperbound and hard cover (case bound). Under paperbound there will be some subcategories.

- *Case bound.* This is the industry term for what we normally call "hard cover." Case bound books can be quite handsome, but they are also more expensive to produce. For the cost of a casebound book you can bring out an entire edition of a modest paperback book or several chapbooks. Most poetry today is published in paperback. There is no really solid marketing reason why you should go with the hard cover option for your book. Currently, the old quality distinction between hard cover and paperback is pretty much gone, with many

HOWL

AND OTHER POEMS

ALLEN GINSBERG

Introduction by William Carlos Williams

Shown here is a facsimile of the cover of Allen Ginsberg's first major book, *Howl and Other Poems*. It is printed in stark black and white and saddle-stitched. The cover is stark, simple, and inexpensive. Publisher-poet Lawrence Ferlinghetti of City Lights Books used this same format for many other titles in his City Lights series, published out of his famous San Francisco bookstore. Such titles were immediately identifiable as City Lights books. In book cover design, you can be dramatic and striking without going overboard with fancy graphics. Simple is always better. Let the poems themselves do the talking.

You can find out all you ever wanted to know about copyright at the Library of Congress web page, and even download the copyright forms you will need to obtain a copyright certificate for your book. The URL is www.loc.gov/copyright/forms.

RECOMMENDED RESOURCE

top-of-the-line books now being published in paper. These books are called "trade paperbacks," as distinct from the throwaway variety that you see on the racks in the supermarkets. This has long been the tradition in Europe.

- *Paperbound.* Paperback books may be perfect-bound or saddle-stitched.

    a. *Perfect-bound books* are like most of those that you see in a bookstore. The covers are usually printed on stiff, shiny (laminated) cover stock. The spine is squared off, and the pages fixed inside with binder's glue. Perfect-bound books vary greatly in quality. Some are very handsome, well-designed books that anyone would be proud to display on a library shelf. The Louisiana State University Press poetry series, one of the finest in the country, is perfect-bound.

    b. *Saddle-stitched books* are held together by staples placed along the spine. Since it normally takes a bulk of 64 or more pages to do a decent perfect binding, books that run shorter than this are often saddle-stitched. This is certainly the most economical way to produce a book. Such a book can be brought out for a few hundred dollars. All chapbooks are saddle-stitched. An acquaintance of mine, the North Carolina poet Mary Belle Campbell, developed a saddle-stitched format for the titles appearing in her poetry series under the Scots Plaid Press imprint. The design of the Scots Plaid books is simple, dignified, and effective. Any poet would be pleased to be published in such

My associate Gary Carbon designed this cover for a collection of poems by Joseph Bathanti, using a single black-and-white photograph and black type. It fit the content (a collection of regional verse), was simple, effective, and inexpensive to print.

a format and, indeed, some very fine poets have been. I am holding in my hand a Scots Plaid Press book called *Rehearsals for Second Endings,* by Eleanor Rodman May. The cover is printed on white cover stock and bears the title, the author's name, and the name and logo of the publisher. The back cover has a picture of the poet and four paragraphs of copy about the poet. Inside the cover is a fly leaf in blue bond, followed by the text itself on white bond. The page size (trim size) is five-and-a-half by eight-and-a-half. This is the standard size of typing and mimeograph paper. The book contains thirty-two pages, plus the cover. Eleanor May's book is a regional title, but many fine, nationally circulated titles have been saddle-stitched. A prime example is the City Lights series published by Lawrence Ferlinghetti. Because of its standard page size a book like this one can be produced in any quick-copy shop—or even on your laser printer. The staples are applied with an inexpensive saddle-stitching (stapling) device available in most large office supply stores. I have one that I paid $14.00 for, and it works for chapbooks up to 32 pages long.

13. Prepare Camera-Ready Copy (Who Sets the Type?)

Your book has to be typeset and made "camera-ready," that is, made ready for the printer to produce printing plates from the material you furnish him. We'll talk more about printers later. For now, let's consider the options for type. The first and best option is for you to do the typesetting yourself. I recommend that you design and typeset your book yourself. It may be a bit dicey at first, and there is a learning curve to contend with, but the long-range benefits of what you will learn are considerable. However, if you do not choose to do this, there are three other options. Whichever of these you choose, you will still have to tell the typesetter precisely how you want your book to look.

1. The printer himself may do the typesetting for you. The downside of this way of handling things is that printers are not book

designers, and will know far less about how to produce an acceptable-looking book than you will, after you read this chapter.

2. You can go to a desktop publisher. These shops utilize the latest computer technology to produce completely designed pages. The quality of their type will vary with the "resolution" capabilities of their equipment. 600 dots per inch has been standard for some years, but newer equipment can produce type with a density of 1200 dots per inch and better. I have found 600 dots per inch quite satisfactory for book production, but if the higher resolution is available and affordable, specify that it be used.

3. You can go to a traditional typography studio. Often these studios have desktop capabilities as well, but they are usually more expensive. They specialize in ad agency and other highly sophisticated work, and they charge a premium price for it.

For either of these sources of type, look in the yellow pages under "typesetting" or "typographers." Prices will vary widely from shop to shop, so always get more than one quote before deciding who will do the job. And I'll remind you again that book design is a very specialized art. Many otherwise competent typographers will not be very experienced at it.

14. Proofread Your Book

After typesetting comes the chore of proofreading. This is a greater challenge than you may think. Good proofreaders are special people, people whose eyes gravitate to errors relentlessly. It is not enough to know the "rules of grammar" or to be a "good speller." I am myself a poor proof reader, even though I taught university-level English for many years. I know the rules. I know how to spell. I just read so fast that I understand meanings and don't see errors.

But, if you don't have a professional proofreader available, what then? Fortunately, there is a technique that will help transform ordinary, literate readers into proof-capable editors. It takes two people to do the job. Here's how it works:

Notes on Chapbook Formats

Some very great poetry has been first published in chapbook form. This kind of publication is well within the financial reach of virtually any writer, and can be quite handsome and striking, in spite of its modest size. Here is Richard Dey again, on chapbook formats.

Today's chapbook is typically between 8 and 32 pages (or two and eight sheets of paper), plus cover; it can be as few as 4 pages or as many as 64; the pages are not usually numbered. They can be miniature in size (4 x 3 inches) or quite large (12 x 9 inches). A slight chapbook can be beefed up by using heavy paper for its interior or adding blank pages at the front and back of the book. It is held together with staples along the fold line, one toward the top and one toward the bottom, or it may be sewn vertically, either by hand with needle and thread or by machine. Often, but not always, the cover is slightly bigger than the book's trim size, and sometimes it extends beyond the fore-edge (the opening edge or edge opposite the binding), so that it is folded at either end into flaps; this makes a handsome item, and resembles a case bound (hardcover) book whose board covers act like borders for the interior pages when opened. A heavier weight paper of a different texture, often colored and coated with some kind of laminate, is used for covers. Uncoated covers tend to soil quickly and badly, but are economical and adequate if protected with acetate or mylar, or even a plastic bag. A high-quality linen or similar cover stock also will withstand misuse, if not dirty hands.

Some chapbooks are further enhanced by regular dust jackets (or "wrappers," as they are known in the trade) so that you do not see the staples embedded in the spine.

—Richard Dey
Poets & Writers Magazine

- Print out two copies of your typeset pages.
- Each reader holds one copy and each has a pencil in hand.
- Take turns reading through the book aloud. While you are reading, your partner follows along in his copy as you read. When an error is noted by either of you, the person not reading pencils in a correction.
- Then your partner does the reading and you take charge of the correcting.
- When you have completed this process, make sure all corrections are noted on a single copy of the printout.
- Make the corrections and do another complete printout.
- Go through the entire process again. Sometimes a correction that you have made can alter a line break, or cause a poem to run over onto a following page, thus spoiling your layout on every page that follows.

15. Decide How Many Books To Print

I recommend that you print a relatively small number of books in the beginning and go back to the printer for more whenever you need them. Such a technique will help you control costs to the point that you should never have to feel that lack of funds is keeping you out of print.

People for whom books are important tend to overestimate the number that can be sold. You may be surprised to learn, for instance, that a first novel by an unknown author may sell fewer than 5,000

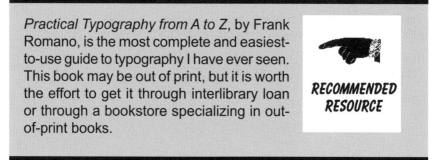

Practical Typography from A to Z, by Frank Romano, is the most complete and easiest-to-use guide to typography I have ever seen. This book may be out of print, but it is worth the effort to get it through interlibrary loan or through a bookstore specializing in out-of-print books.

RECOMMENDED RESOURCE

copies—if that many—even when it is promoted nationwide by a major publisher with a national sales staff.

How do you estimate the number of books that you should print? Here's a case history that may help you decide. I recently published a city-county pictorial history of the town of Greenville, North Carolina. Such books are strong sells, and typically have a far greater number of potential buyers than a volume of poetry.

At the time of publication, Greenville had approximately 38,000 inhabitants and 12,000 households. Of the 12,000 households, I reasoned, half never read anything at all, leaving 6,000. Of this number at least half never read anything but the newspaper, leaving 3,000. Of the remaining 3,000 half read only mass market paperbacks and no history books, leaving 1,500 potential customers. Of this 1,500 half might want my book but would have no money to buy it with, leaving 750. Of the 750 with both the desire and the money to read my book, a certain number would simply not get around to making the purchase. And there would always be others who—in spite of all my efforts—would never even know that the book existed.

I decided to print 500, believing that I could sell 300 immediately and the remaining 200 over a reasonable period of time. And this is precisely what happened.

I would suggest—and most of those I have consulted agree with me—that an initial edition of 300 copies is entirely adequate. If you use a quick-copy shop or a short run printer, you would do well to consider an edition as small as 100 copies.

Very limited editions are possible for saddle-stitched books. For perfect bound books, the press set up and the bindery set up constitute a major portion of the cost, and this will be the same no matter how many or how few copies you print.

16. Get a Quote from Several Printers

One of the main things to remember is that there is no standard price for book production. Always get several quotes from different printers. There are small print shops in every town that are capable of bringing out a saddle-stitched book. Even better are the "copy shops" that cater "to the trade," that is, to publishers and other businesses who

---

Request for Quote Form

Name of book or publication:

Quantity:

Trim Size:

Number of Pages:

Text Stock:

Cover Stock:

Halftones:

Binding:

     ❑ Casebound

     ❑ Saddle-stitched

     ❑ Perfect bound

Estimated turnaround time:

Freight:

Delivered to: _____

    Please return your quote on the above job ASAP to:

    (Your Name and Address).

Typefaces have long and fascinating histories, starting with Gutenburg's first movable type in the late 14th century. Aficionados of typography know these histories and choose typefaces with the fastidious discrimination of the artist.

buy at wholesale prices. In South Florida, where I live, there are retail shops like Kinko's or Ikon who will charge as much as four or five dollars for a modest chapbook. The wholesale printer I use can do the job for $1.50. The only way to find the printer you need for saddle-stitched books is to get on the telephone and go down the list.

Perfect-bound books and case bound books, however, are best handled by specialty book printers. Unless you are lucky enough to live near such a printer (there is a cluster of them, for instance, in the Ann Arbor area) you will be dealing with an out-of-town firm.

Get lots of quotes. Prices from printers can vary by as much as 200% (and more) for the same job. It is very bad business indeed not to get competitive quotes and choose among them. How do you find these printers? Well, get on the internet and do a Yahoo search for "short-run printers." There are three that I have used and that I can recommend. Contact information is given below:

- The first of these shops is Bookcrafters, 140 Buchanan Street, Chelsea, Michigan, 48118. Just call them at (313) 475-9145 and tell them you want a quote on a printing job.
- The second printer is McNaughton & Gunn, P.O. Box M2060, Ann Arbor, MI 48106. The telephone number is (313) 429-5411.
- You can also give a call to Technical Communications at 112 West 12th Avenue, North Kansas City, MO, 64116. The telephone number is (816) 842-9770.
- Lightning Print of La Vergne Tennessee has new equipment that can turn out perfect bound books one at a time at a very reasonable cost after setup charges are paid. However, their presses will not produce books of fewer than 104 pages. The address is 1246 Heil-Quaker Blvd., La Vergne, TN 37086. You can call them at (615) 287-5103.

Remember that your poem is the star of the show, and that the book that contains it should put nothing whatsoever between the reader and the direct enjoyment of your verse. Well-written poetry does not need decoration. It is its own decoration.

How Much Will It Cost?

Can you afford to bring out your own book or will you be wasting your time even thinking about it? Here are some recent examples from my own business:

- 100 copies of a 64-page, saddle-stitched book printed at local copy shop was $164. Typography cost another $150 (Remember, you can do this yourself on your computer and save this expense). Miscellaneous costs were, say, $100. Total cost for the edition: $414. The book retails for $7.95.
- 500 copies printed with a laminated cover, perfect bound at Bookcrafters cost me $1,200. This book was 48 pages long. Type cost another $200. I paid a photographer $100 for the cover shot. The book sold at retail for $9.95. Cost for the project: $1280.
- I am currently producing 500 copies of a case bound book, 164 pages long. Printing and binding are going to cost $2,050. I set my own type, but if I had hired it out it would have cost $33 to $500.

Somewhere within this range you will find a cost level suitable to your book and to your pocketbook. Believe me, no great prestige attaches to expensively bound books. It is the quality of the poetry within that is going to make or break your book, so long as the overall design is done with taste and professionalism.

The Single Most Important Question

When you have done everything else you can do; when you have adjusted the print run to the most economical level, chosen the paper with an eye toward cost, typeset, and laid out your own publication, contacted several printers and secured multiple quotes, there is still one more absolutely essential step. With his quote in hand, give your printer a call. Tell him that you are just about ready to make a commitment, but that his price, though good, is just a bit beyond your budget. "Can you," you ask him, "see any way that I can get this down just a bit?" Specify here just how much of a reduction you're looking for.

Well, maybe he can help you and maybe he can't. But in a surprising number of cases, the printer will come up with some money-saving ideas. He will do this because he wants and needs your business. He may do this for any one of a variety of reasons:

- His shop is empty, a customer has just delayed a job, and his pressmen are standing around without anything much to do.
- He quoted you a bit high in the first place just to see what the traffic would bear. Now he knows, and he will come down a bit to please you.
- He really does know a way to get the price down a bit.

Book Design Checklist

• Choose the poems you wish to include.

• Name your book.

• Determine page size (trim size).

• Choose the paper you want to print your book on.

• Select the typeface you wish to use.

• Design a typical page.

• Determine the sequence of your poems.

• Prepare the front matter.

• Decide how long your book will be.

• Design the front and back cover.

• Decide on the kind of binding you want.

• Typeset your book.

• Proofread your book.

• Prepare camera-ready copy or disk file.

• Decide how many to print.

• Get quotes from printers.

Summary of Typographical Recommendations

- Never use more than two type families in the same book.

- Always choose modest, readable fonts. Fancy scripts, one of the many varieties of "Old English," and similar fonts are taboo in good book design.

- The text should normally be set in 10, 11, or 12 point type.

- Use two, three, or four points of leading between the lines.

- Typeset the title two points larger than the text.

- The title can be made distinct from the text by setting in caps the same size as the text, or setting it in upper and lower case italic or roman two point sizes larger than the text.

- Use twice as much leading between the title and the first line of the poem as you used in the text.

- When a line is "run over," that is, too long to be displayed as a single line, indent the run over portion of the line at least one quarter inch more than any normal indent in your poem.

- Poems may be set centered on the longest line, flush left, or flush left with an indention.

- Do not crowd poems onto the page. Leave each poem in its own white space so that it can capture the attention of the reader.

Chapter Eight / How to Start and Publish Your Own Poetry Series

Once you've brought out your own book and learned the basics of publishing and selling poetry, you can easily extend your activities to include publishing the work of other good poets. In so doing, you will be performing a real service to your fellow poets and doing yourself a favor, too. Your life will be enriched by the poems and poets you love so well. As the editor and publisher of your own poetry series, a great store of personal satisfaction lies ahead for you. And, of course, there will be work, too.

Publishing is Fun

Why should you do this? For many reasons, not the least of which is that being a publisher is a lot of fun for anyone who loves books.

- Your social and professional life will take a dramatic turn for the better. You will continually meet interesting people and read good poetry (and, alas, some very bad poetry).
- You will develop a very large circle of friends in the literary and arts communities.
- You will become a leader in the literary activities of your region or state.
- You will be one of those who make things happen in the arts in general.
- You can develop a high public visibility that will put you at the center of the kinds of activities that are meaningful to you.
- The days and years of isolation, of trying to find somebody, somewhere, to talk to about poetry will be over once and for all.
- In the long run, you may even decide, as you learn the ropes, to publish a little magazine or works of fiction (the hardest of all

to sell) and non-fiction (the easiest to market and sell).

- With modest effort you can become one of the important facilitators of the art of poetry in your region. Poets need publishers, especially good ones who understand what poems are all about.

You Learn As You Go

Is all this impossibly difficult? Does it require years of training or a lengthy apprenticeship? It does not. I found when I jumped into the business with no more experience than you have, that publishing is a little like raising a family. You don't know anything at all about it when you start out, but you learn very quickly as you go. After all, your progress can be as slow or as quick as you wish. You don't have to bring out any more titles each year than you are comfortable with.

You will soon find that it becomes routine, and that you can easily handle the many details that will confront you.

No Financial Burden

In addition you need not have any money at all at risk. Remember that most books of verse can be published quite inexpensively. Since the writers themselves will participate in these costs, there will be virtually no financial pressure on you, as publisher, that you do not voluntarily assume. The poets themselves will be doing most of the hands-on marketing and selling, since that's the only way that poetry will sell, in any case.

Publishing poetry may not cost much money, but it will surely cost *something*. Where are the funds to come from?

- *Your own money.* You do not want to risk your own money publishing other people's poetry. Your own poetry, OK, but that of others, no. There may be some exceptions in the case of poets with very strong bookselling track records, but these will be few and far between, and I advise you in any case to look at them very carefully. You will be investing a good deal of time in the project, anyway. And there are incidental overhead expenses. There's the telephone, the portion of the utilities you allocate to your publishing activities, random stamps and stationery, some limited travel expense—and it all adds up. No, get the money for actually typesetting, printing, and selling the book from somewhere else. For example....

- *Your poet's money.* Ask your authors to invest in themselves, just as you were advised to do in Chapter Two to get your own work published. It is quite acceptable today to get author participation in defraying these direct production expenses, as well as any general overhead expenses (do not neglect to include these) that you may not be able or willing to meet yourself. In return, the poet gets your book editing, design and marketing skills, as well as the prestige of appearing over your carefully protected and widely respected imprint.

- *Grant money and art council money.* But there is another possibility, and that is the use of OPM, or "other people's money." No bank will lend you any money, of course, on such a hare-brained (from the traditional banking point of view) venture as that of publishing poetry, and no investors will come beating your door down for a piece of the action, either. But there are other sources, principally local and state arts councils. As you establish yourself and gain more visibility, it will become more and more feasible to finance your publishing activities with grant money from such public or quasi-public agencies. To qualify for such funds you may have to organize your operation as a not-for-profit corporation. This does not mean that you can't get paid or earn money for your services. It just means that the corporation itself doesn't earn money and issue dividends to shareholders. Profits after expenses (including reasonable salaries) must be plowed back into the activities defined in the corporate charter as those approved for your organization to engage in. Businesses, industries, and individuals can also be invited to contribute to non-profit corporations. Such contributions are tax deductible. Some attorneys will contribute their services to set up such corporations when they themselves are interested in its activities.

Getting Started

Getting started as a publisher is really quite easy, once you make up your mind to do so. Essentially, you simply begin to do for others what you have learned to do for yourself. The very fact that you are reading this book and learning how to market and sell poetry means that you are, at heart, a more outgoing and take-charge person than others who would not be willing or able to take on such leadership responsibilities.

An Editorial Board?

Many poetry series are the work of a single individual, and that is what I recommend to you as you start out. However, at some point you may find it advantageous to have a volunteer "editorial board." The board may have as many or as few duties as its members are willing to undertake and you are willing to delegate. The advantage of this board is that it takes the burden off any single individual when it comes time to accept or, especially, reject manuscripts. An editorial board should have as members established poets or other literary persons with as much public visibility as possible. Such board members can enhance your visibility and create some literary clout. They can also help attract submissions from the more serious and accomplished poets. However, you, as editor-in-chief, should retain the authority to make all final decisions. Should you decide to organize as a not-for-profit corporation then the editorial board of directors becomes a legal necessity.

Priming the Pump

The first few titles you bring out are very important to the success of your series. Work hard to get the most solid, well-wrought verse that you can. Don't wait for manuscripts to come to you; solicit submissions from poets whose names you respect and whose works will provide a firm foundation for works to come, which may well be by unknown or emerging poets.

Limit your contacts to those whose work is almost sure to be good enough to appear in your series. Carry on this editorial prospecting quietly, and without publicity. You may have very good friends who write very poor poetry, and you don't want to alienate these people. Once you get first rate work out, others will see it and be able to measure their own efforts against it and know whether they are in or out of your league.

And here's a bit of advice about dealing with writers, something I had to learn the hard way. When you evaluate a manuscript and respond to the person who submitted it, say precisely what you mean. Most of us have had the experience—at writer's groups and critique sessions, say—of hiding our real opinions about poems being read to avoid hurting the feelings of some especially sensitive person.

As an editor and publisher you no longer have this luxury. You can be tactful, but you must speak the truth. When I was new in the business I often returned manuscripts in their SASE with some innocuous phrase like, "I like these but they need more work. Better luck next time." You need to understand that the hopeful poet will understand such words to mean "Polish these a bit and I'll publish them. They're great."

It's not necessary to be harsh, but if you are rejecting a collection of poems, say so: "Thank you for letting me read these. I'm afraid I can't accept them for Orpheus Press, but good luck with them elsewhere."

If you really are on the fence, be specific in your criticisms. If you want the author to make some changes or rework some poems tell him so, but make it clear that he will be doing this *on speculation* and that you cannot promise to accept them once the work is done. In matters of editorial decision making *there is absolutely no substitute for clarity.*

Your Quality Is Your Stock-in-Trade: Protect It at All Costs

As a literary publisher, your reputation is of prime importance and must be maintained at all costs. One of the things you must do is to watch over the quality of your list of published books with great vigilance. Books, like people, are judged by the company they keep. This is especially true of reviewers and critics. This is why the so-called "vanity presses" can't even buy a review in any reputable publication. Even should they, through sheer luck, publish an occasional book of merit, it is submerged in the avalanche of trash represented by the other titles on their list.

Don't accept any book, even one by a close friend, that is not up to your standard. An editorial review board may act as a buffer for you in accepting and rejecting manuscripts.

> Watch over the quality of your list of published books with great vigilance. Books, like people, are judged by the company they keep. You can publish Aunt Minnie's doggerel if you wish. This may keep peace in the family, but the reputation of the good poets on your list and that of your press will suffer by the association.

Choose a Strong Name for Your Series

Be sure that the name you choose for your poetry series will reflect the nature of the poetry you intend to publish and also possess all the marketing and public relations strength possible. If you plan a series of regional poets, then link your series to the region through its title. This will help get you onto bookstore shelves devoted to local and regional authors, help you set up readings, and give focus and identity to your publishing effort. If your series will publish poems about a place or region, then let its name reflect that relationship. There is an endless number of specialties: new and emerging voices, feminist poems, new age and metaphysical poems, cowboy poems, and too many more to list. Whatever your slant, let it be reflected in the name of your series.

Design a Distinctive Cover

Your covers should be immediately recognizable as belonging to your poetry series. I discussed some of the imperatives of successful covers in the last chapter, and that discussion is still relevant here. So you already know that your cover should be direct, simple, and affordable. When you design the cover for your series, incorporate in it the following qualities:

- Even the most cursory glance at the cover will identify it as belonging to your series. You want to gain name recognition and a reputation for quality. If you have brought out a book or two by well-known poets, then something of their luster will rub off on later books in the series by virtue of the constant cover design.

- The name of your poetry series should be displayed on the cover, subordinate to the title and the author's name, but nonetheless prominent.

Your Production and Marketing Schedule

You will need a general publication and marketing schedule for use with every title you publish. There is no need to reinvent your publishing methods and procedures for each book as it comes along. Such a schedule will make it far easier to handle the details, fully and in order, that publishing entails.

Promotional Contacts and Mailing Lists

Develop a file of publicity outlets, review sources, and bookstore special events coordinators. This will be an ever-growing, ever-changing list. As you add new names, update older listings, prune dead end leads, and highlight the most useful ones, the list will become more and more valuable to you.

You may have a database program that will handle the compiling of mailing lists and contact lists for you. If not, or if you find the one you have too complex, there are simple programs on the shelves that will do the job for you. I use one called "My Mail List." It is available for Mac and Windows. I paid $37 for my copy.

Whenever possible include the actual name of your contact. Instead of "Book Editor" or "Review Editor," try always to list "John Jones, Book Editor" or "Mary Smith, Review Editor." Include street addresses, email addresses, telephone numbers, and fax numbers.

Once you have made your list of contacts, develop and cultivate it. Never miss an opportunity to send a news item or tip to a book editor or lifestyle editor. Send complimentary letters when someone on your contact list writes something memorable, gets a promotion, or performs in an outstanding way. Send birthday cards and holiday greeting

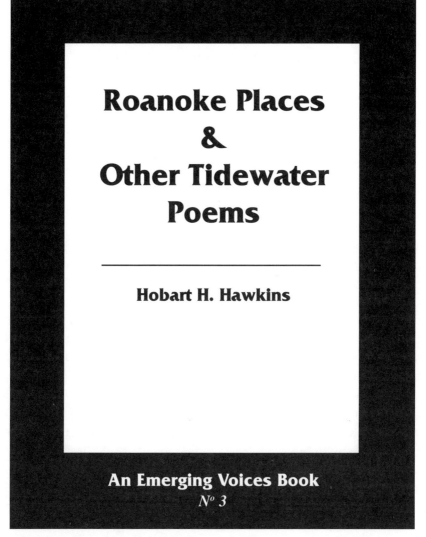

Roanoke Places
&
Other Tidewater
Poems

Hobart H. Hawkins

An Emerging Voices Book
N° 3

This sample book cover could scarcely be more simple, yet it embodies all the elements of successful poetry series design. It is simple and economical, yet striking and easy to remember. The title and the author are clearly displayed, legible from a reasonable distance. The series name is prominently placed as a reverse at the bottom of the cover. The use of "N° 3" reveals at once that this book is a part of an ongoing series.

cards. Treat them the way you would like them to treat you and your authors.

Develop a Standard Author-Publisher Contract

Contracts for a poetry series are simpler than for a non-fiction book or a novel. There are no book club rights, movie and television rights or translation rights to contend with. Nevertheless, the agreement that you reach with your author will be formal, and it will be signed. It will specify all the things that you, as publisher, will do for the author:

You will also specify what your author will do for you: he will pay you a subsidy of a certain amount; he will do this at a specifically appointed time; he will actively market his book (be as detailed as possible); he will warrant that he has utilized no copyrighted materials and will hold you harmless in case of litigation over copyright infringement; and so on. You will find examples of publishing contracts in Richard Balkin's *An Author's Guide to Book Publishing* and in Judith Appelbaum's *How to Get Happily Published*. These standard contracts contain far more provisions than you will need, but you can pick and choose among them. There is also an excellent short contract in publishing consultant John Huenefeld's *Guide to Book Publishing,* a basic how-to guide to the entire publishing field. If these books and others recommended later are not in your library they can be readily obtained through an interlibrary loan request.

A simple publishing agreement is reproduced at the end of this chapter. It is straightforward, easy to understand, and covers all of the necessary bases. I developed it after studying many contracts, including those offered to me by university presses and other publishers who were contracting with me to publish my own books. I then had my attorney review and approve it. You should use this model, plus the others I have mentioned, to draw up your own agreement, adding anything that may be unique to the way you have organized your business. Then have an attorney review the agreement for you. For your information, my Venture Press contract is reproduced on pages 103 and 104.

Steps to Publication

Once you have decided to publish a given book, enter its name

Book Marketing Checklist

(The following checklist takes you through each step
in a complete marketing plan.)

* Assign ISBN through R.R. Bowker. This will list your book in all national and international databases utilized by the book trade.
* Set publication date.
* Prepare production and publication schedule.
* Send ABI (Advance Book Information) form to R.R. Bowker.
* Get bar code.
* Have author fill out author information form and send in photographs.
* Prepare media kit.
    —photo
    —news release(s)
    —fact sheet
    —bookstore PR author forms
    —reply card
    —copies of reviews
* Design and typeset text.
* Design and typeset covers. When galleys are ready, have bound galleys made.
* Send galleys for blurbs and reviews.
* Mount pre-publication sales campaign.
* When printed copies are received, send to review sources listed above; in addition, send review copies to newspapers and magazines nationwide.
* Send media kit & book to major media.
* Identify and contact specialty markets and catalogues.

> You can save a great deal of money on legal fees by being well-prepared before you enter the attorney's office. Remember, the attorney knows less about your business than you do. Always have a sample document prepared and hand it over for review, rather than saying something vague like "I need a contract." Attorneys charge by the minute and the clock is ticking from the minute you walk in. Even small talk is going to cost you $125 or more an hour.

atop your production and marketing schedule and begin to work your way down the list, checking each item off as you go. The checklist I use is shown on the previous page. There is plenty of room to add other items that you find desirable.

Share this plan with your author. The poet will be excited about the upcoming publication of his book, and will be ready to jump in and do whatever he can to help. Assign the author particular duties, such as developing a media kit and bookstore PR form. You can redesign and reformat as necessary the promotional material the writer submits, but you cannot easily do all the detail work of digging up the relevant facts. The writer will also make a list of review sources that you may not know about and list other poets or writers to whom proofs of his work can be sent for the purpose of eliciting endorsements and comments that can be printed on the back cover of the book. Then start at the top and follow through on your plan, checking items off as you go.

The Importance of Networking

When you decide to set out on the fascinating road toward becoming a publisher, no one book will tell you everything you need or want to know. You will complete that information by learning from the experience and wisdom of those who have gone that way before you. Publishers love to talk about publishing, poets love to talk about poetry and publishers of poetry love to talk about both. You will find that there is a rich network of small press people out there, nearly all of whom will be more than happy to talk to you. Just pick up the phone and call.

When I decided to publish a weekly newspaper in the college town of Davidson, North Carolina (in which I published poetry, by the way), I had absolutely no experience in the newspaper business. I began to visit the shops of other weeklies in neighboring towns. At every one of them I was welcomed not only as a business colleague, but as a kindred soul. The information and experience that came my way from the sources would prove invaluable—even essential—to me.

Attend writers' conferences and seek out other self-publishers and small press publishers who will also be there. Exchange ideas, techniques and serendipitous solutions to day-to-day problems that have come your way.

The internet, through its network of World Wide Web pages, provides instant communication with others who share your interests and activities. Subscribe to mailing lists. Participate in news groups. Visit key sites regularly.

Continue to read widely in the field, especially firsthand accounts of literary adventurers like yourself.

This agreement, made this sixth day of _____ by and between _____, hereinafter referred to as "author," and Thomas A. Williams, Editor-in-chief, Venture Press, hereinafter referred to as "publisher," for the publication of the book entitled _____ hereinafter referred to as "the work,"

W I T N E S S E T H

PART I:

1. Publisher agrees to edit, design, print, and market (as specified below) a first edition of _____ copies of the work, including cover, as follows:

a. Said work shall consist of no more than _____ printed pages.

b. Said work shall consist of pages ___ by ____ inches in size.

c. Said work shall be printed on _____ stock.

d. Said work shall be bound in _____ cover stock.

2. Publisher shall obtain an ISBN number and have said work listed in Books in Print and other national catalogues, listings and databases.

3. Publisher shall provide to the author a valid certificate of copyright. Copyright will be registered in the name of the author.

4. Publisher shall have the right to sell the work through retail outlets for the duration of this agreement. For the purposes of this contract, the "duration of this agreement" refers to the time required to sell the initial printing of _____ copies or _____ year(s), whichever is earlier. After the first edition is sold out, any further agreement between the author and the publisher shall be at the option of the author.

5. Publisher shall furnish to author galley proofs and final page proofs. <u>Author agrees to proofread galley and page proofs and approve final proofs for printing</u>. Publisher shall also proofread the typeset work.

PART II:

1. The author shall receive from the publisher monies and royalties as follows:

a. On all books sold directly by the author or the author's agents to individual buyers at professional events or in any other way, or to libraries or other organizations or individuals, the author shall retain 20% of the proceeds of said sale.

b. On books sold by the publisher at retail or through jobbers, wholesalers or distributors, publisher shall pay to the author a royalty of 20% of the net proceeds of the sale. "Net Proceeds" means all monies actually received by the publisher as a result of these sales, less make-goods and returns.

c. For book club rights, reprint rights or foreign rights, the publisher shall pay to the author 60% of the net proceeds for the purchase of rights. Sixty percent of subsequent royalties deriving from these sales shall be paid to the author.

d. There shall be a clear accounting to the author of all monies received by the publisher from the sale of the work. Such accountings shall take place annually, in August. Payment of all royalties due the author shall be made in full at the time of each such accounting.

e. The publisher shall furnish to the author _____ copies of the work at no cost for the author's personal use and distribution.

PART III:

1. Author agrees to pay to the publisher the sum of $_____ as follows: One third of

the total shall be paid on the signing of this contract; one-third shall be paid on the submission to the author of galley proofs; and one third shall be paid on the submission to the author of page proofs.

2. Author's alterations (discretionary changes in the text made by the author after initial typesetting) will be billed to the author at the rate of $____ an hour.

3. Author agrees to furnish to publisher the text of the work on computer disk in a standard word processing format.

4. Complete responsibility for the infringement (by plagiarism, libel, or other means) of the rights of others by material included in the original manuscript shall be borne by the author, who shall hold the publisher harmless in any such action.

5. Both the author and the publisher agree that sales of said work cannot be guaranteed.

Part IV:

1. The author agrees to assist the publisher actively in the promotion of the work in the implementation of the marketing schedule prepared for the work, as requested by the publisher.

2. The author agrees to make every effort to arrange readings, participate in open mike sessions, appear at bookstore signings and to engage in other activities, at every opportunity, that will encourage and increase sales of the work.

3. This contract is the entire agreement between the publisher and the author concerning the publication of the work.

Part V:

Other terms and conditions, if any:

Acceptance of this agreement:

_____

John Doe, Author

_____

Thomas A. Williams, Ph.D., Editor-in-chief, Venture Press

Note: I furnish this sample agreement as an example only. If you think it may work for you, adapt it to your needs and take it to your attorney for review.

Chapter Nine / The Unabashed Poet's Guide to Self-Promotion and Publicity

Your poems and books of poems will sell, but you must make them sell. I don't mean that you have to hawk them like the guy pushing sausage sandwiches at the state fair, though that beats not selling them at all. While you can bring your book to market with professionalism and dignity, you must also do it as energetically and as aggressively as your personality will permit. You will have to blow your own horn a bit. If you don't, no one else will. Other people have horns of their own to worry about. Sometimes you can do this behind the scenes by making it possible and very easy for other people to do the blowing for you. For instance:

- Articles about you and your work will appear in newspapers and magazines so long as you carefully write the releases and send them out regularly.
- A review may blow your horn for you so long as you put the horn (a copy of your book and your media kit) into the reviewer's hands.
- Autograph parties and readings will be rousing successes so long as you carefully schedule, organize, and stage them. (These are such important events that a separate chapter will be devoted to each of them.)

You must understand and accept the fact that if you want to be known as a poet, you will have to take steps to make yourself known as a poet. Don't underrate the importance of following this prescription for building literary success through building a literary reputation. Walt Whitman saw the need and did what was necessary. Without his systematic self-promotion, *Leaves of Grass* might have remained a manuscript in a bureau drawer. Bill Henderson tells the story in his

Publish-It-Yourself Handbook: Literary Tradition and How-To:

"Walt Whitman not only had some artistic know-how, he also knew how to wheel and deal. In 1855 he himself set the type for *Leaves of Grass* on the press of Andrew and James Rome in Brooklyn: ninety-five pages, twelve poems, somewhat under a thousand books. He got his review copies out and attracted some notice, but he wrote the best reviews himself... The copy he sent to Emerson brought a less prejudiced rave. Emerson's letter in reply stated, 'I am not blind to the worth of the wonderful gift of *Leaves of Grass*. I find it the most extraordinary piece of wit and wisdom that America has yet contributed. I am very happy in reading it, as great power makes us happy...I greet you at the beginning of a great career...' Without Emerson's permission, Whitman splashed, 'I greet you at the beginning of a great career—Emerson,' in gold on the back of his next edition."

That is a very small part of what Walt Whitman had to do to promote one of the greatest poems in the English language. Who are you to shrink back from this kind of work on behalf of your own verse?

> *He who has*
> *A thing to sell,*
> *And goes and*
> *whispers in a well,*
> *Is not so apt*
> *To get the dollars,*
> *As he who climbs*
> *A tree and hollers.*
> *—Barbara Brabec*
> Homemade Money

Reputations are Made, Not Born

While there are exceptions to every generalization, you can accept it as 99.99% true that there are no reputations in any field that are not made reputations. Don't count on the good fairy to do for things that you are unwilling to do for yourself. The good fairy is notoriously unreliable, and will seldom take time to fulfill your basic needs, much less your fondest expectations. The personal, professional, and even financial rewards which will come to the writer who sees to his own publicity are substantial indeed. As a poet, you and you alone are the chief

Bill Henderson's classic *The Publish-It-Yourself Handbook* is a great read and inspiration for poets and other small press writers and publishers.

RECOMMENDED RESOURCE

marketer of your wares. This chore is not unique to the publication of poetry. It is well known in the publishing industry that, except for very rare exceptions, only hard promotional work on the part of the writer will keep even the most potentially saleable books on the market long enough to become successful. Wayne Dyer is said to have loaded case after case of *Your Erroneous Zones* into the trunk of his car and took off on a self-sponsored, cross-country tour. James Redfield sold *The Celestine Prophecy* on his own for many years before it was picked by Time-Warner and hit the big time.

While poets are not dealing with such big bucks, and while blockbuster commercial success is almost certainly out of their reach, their bookselling efforts are just as essential to their success, or even more so. Just one more example: One poet I know recently sold 100 of his books just after they came off the press. The book had a regional theme, and he sold this large batch to the county development commission, which uses them to highlight cultural activities in the area when they make their pitch to top industrial clients. The money from this one sale came close to paying the out-of-pocket printing costs.

The development commission did not come to the poet. He went to the commission. Had he waited, alone in his study, for the hordes to come knocking at his door and demanding his product, no sale would even have been made. He did not wait. He acted on his idea. He made it happen. This same poet scheduled a series of readings (see the chapter "How to Sell Your Books at a Poetry Reading," below) at which he sold even more books. He has entered his book in state competitions, been reviewed in top newspapers, and used his book to land jobs teaching creative writing at community colleges. Notice that I use the active

It's Time to Take Action

Have you ever wondered why the names of the same writers seem to appear in local and regional anthologies, magazines, and small press reviews over and over again; why the same people are always appointed to arts commissions, asked to give talks and write introductions, participate in arts festival programs, get appointed to state arts posts, give talks at yearly writers' group meetings?

It's not a matter of luck, nor is it a coincidence that these names appear so frequently on "noted writer" lists. It's just that these people have managed, one way or another, to create a public visibility adequate to build a literary reputation. When organizers or grant givers fish around for the name of a "poet" for some purpose or other, they naturally choose among those that they have heard about. Don't waste time complaining about this; accept it. It is simply the nature of the world.

Why, you ask, do they keep overlooking me? You know that you have ideas, talent, and a generous heart, and much to give. You'd like not only to be a poet, but a recognized poet, as well. If you have heard that still, small voice of longing to be better known murmuring deep within you, you are not alone. Most of us will not rush to admit it, but the voice is there all the same.

If we want to become a part of this higher echelon, we must let people know who and what we are, and that we are ready to take on our share of the (joyful) burden. It is time to blow your own horn a little. There is no ostentation here, no unjustified self-aggrandizement. It is just a matter of taking the simple and gentle steps that will insure your success as a writer.

Bill Henderson, founder of Pushcart Press, warned that many books are unknown because an "otherwise talented author . . . has insufficient enthusiasm and endurance in proclaiming his work to the public."

If this describes you, it's time to take action.

voice. The author *did* these things. They were not done to him or for him. Contrary to what our mothers may have told us, nature does not really care whether we succeed in our endeavors or not. The atmospheric pressure at sea level and the rate of acceleration due to gravity are totally indifferent to our collective and individual fates. No, there's nothing out there that is going to do it for us. We succeed only when we harness our own brains, energies, and talents and do the things we have to do to succeed.

Prepare a Media Kit

The first step is to prepare a media kit. These used to be called "press kits," as though television didn't exist, but no more. The media kit is your most important information packet, and it is designed to make the work of those from whom you hope to get coverage that much easier.

Each item in it will have multiple uses. Sometimes you will send the complete kit. Sometimes you will send only the news release or some other single item.

A complete media kit will contain the following items:

- A fact sheet on yourself as author. This fact sheet will include a short bio of you, a listing of your credits, short excerpts from favorable reviews or interviews, a statement of your goals and motivations as a writer, quotable quotes, etc. Keep it in easily utilized, outline form so that a feature writer or reviewer can find and excerpt materials that are needed for a write-up.
- In preparing this fact sheet, as in preparing all the other marketing materials in your repertoire, bear in mind that reporters—whether print or electronic—will not have time to research an article on you and your work. You have to do this for them. When your fact sheet is well done and easily utilized, you take a giant step toward getting the kind of publicity you need. The fact sheet can also be used as a background piece to include in your poetry submissions to magazines and to publishers. It can be given to program chairmen who

have to introduce you to audiences before whom you are scheduled to appear. You can have it blown up to poster size and use it as a prop at readings, autograph parties, and other occasions.

- Your media kit will also include a fact sheet on your book. What press published it? How many pages? What about special themes? What about quotes to illustrate these themes? How can the book be obtained? At what price? Your book fact sheet may well include an item or two that also appears on your personal fact sheet. Don't worry about necessary duplication, but don't repeat materials needlessly.

- Clips of any pre-publication or other reviews (or interviews) that you may have had. You will photocopy these and keep them readily available.

- Copies of any other articles that may have been written about you or by you.

- A brief news release of one full page or less, a short, straightforward story telling that you wrote your book and that it was published.

- A complete feature article of 500 to 700 words, with photographs. This piece is a personality profile of you and your work. Will the article be used? Sometimes it will and sometimes it won't. It all depends on the space availability and intrinsic interest of your article. One thing, though, is certain. It will certainly not be used if you do not write it and send it out. Most newspapers are understaffed and do not have a regular book review editor. Some writers will use your article as a guide. Some newspapers—especially weeklies, which will be happy to have a free feature—will print it just as you provide it. Always manage to tell readers how and where they can buy your book. Include a mention of your publishing company: "My Book of Poems was published by Muse Books of Tupelo, Mississippi." Also include a mention of the retail price.

- Include a glossy, black and white photograph of yourself. Some kind of action shot in a natural surrounding will get a better play than a simple mug shot since it will have greater reader

How to Get Productive Again

Writer's block got you down? I suffered an acute case for many years. As a writer, I was my own worst enemy. Then I read Dorothea Brande, where I found this simple bit of advice. "Act as though it were impossible to fail," Dorothea advised.

For years, like some malevolently negative parrot perched on my own shoulder, I constantly fed messages into my ear. "You call that writing?" I would say to myself. Or, "That's the sorriest stuff I ever saw." Or, "Nobody in his right mind would call that poetry." Naturally, this didn't help at all. Then I began to play Dorothea Brande's game. I didn't have to believe it, I simply had to *act* as though I believed it. I began to write as though it were impossible not to write good, strong lines. And you know what? I began to write more of them than I had ever been able to do before.

Another bit of advice that has been immensely helpful to me: Brande reminded me that "You can't create and criticize simultaneously." When you're constantly criticizing every word you put down on the page, you simply stifle the free flow of words, images, and rhythms. It's like trying to water the daisies when there's a kink in the hose. There's plenty of water in the pipe, but only a dribble comes out the nozzle. Shake the kink out and water flows freely. That's what happens when you shake out the mental kinks of constant self-criticism.

There's time enough to exercise your critical faculties after you get the first draft down on paper.

interest. If you are writing a poem about your conquest of Mt. Everest, the photograph ought to show you on the summit.

Send Out Review Copies

Don't be stingy with review copies. Don't waste them, of course, but do send one to every publication that you feel might review your book. The cost of sending these copies will be one of the best investments you make.

Send your media kit along with your book to weekly newspapers and smaller dailies. For major dailies with a regular book reviewer, send a book along with a picture and your fact sheet.

There may be periodicals and radio and TV stations that you truly feel are marginal. In these cases, you may not want to send a copy of your book. Instead, send a cover letter, a personal fact sheet, and a reply card for use in requesting a review copy. When a card from such a mailing comes in, send a copy of your book, personally addressed to the individual who requested the review copy. Include your fact sheets, again, with the book. You may also elect to send your complete media kit with the review copy.

Important: Everything that you send out should be on the publishing company letterhead. The review package should come from the publisher (that's you as publisher or someone else as publisher) rather than from you personally.

The exception to this rule comes when you know the reviewer personally or when you have personal contacts at your local newspaper. In such cases you can hand deliver the package or arrange a lunch date at which you can better pitch your product.

If you do an autograph signing, or if there is some celebration of the publication of your book, a good black-and-white photograph showing you at the occasion could make it into print when you live in a relatively small town. Such a photograph is not likely to get much attention on its own in a major metropolitan area.

Your local library will have a reference book containing lists of contact persons and addresses of the media, large and small. Always address your review material to an individual, by name, whenever possible.

Small but Powerful Promotional Publications

Do not overlook association newsletters, organizational magazines, and other second-line publications. These can be a great help in creating the kind of public recognition that you are after.

If there are other tie-ins, be sure to exploit them. If your poetry commemorates some historical occasion, and if you are a member of the DAR, for instance, send a package to the organization's magazine or newsletter editor. If you are a member of the American Legion and your poetry has a patriotic theme, send a copy to the *American Legion Magazine*. You won't hit many of the national publications at the right time, and you will have to understand that the competition for limited space is fierce. But take advantage of every possibility. You will not get your message into print every time you attempt to do so, but when you do succeed, the results can be very important to you. You can ask to have a copy of any review sent to you, but, normally, this is not done. You will not know of reviews in papers you don't regularly read until some acquaintance tells you, casually, "Hey, I read that article about your book in the paper last week."

Bombard the World with News Releases

You will not want to send your complete media kit to everyone. It is too expensive. But you should send a news release to every possible source of publicity.

Do news releases work? You bet they do. Some time back I organized a small publishing company to bring out a commercial magazine. Everything worked fine, except for one thing. Since I was new in business, the printer wanted to be paid in advance. Yet I could not collect from my advertisers until I had the published magazine in hand. Where was I going to get the $20,000 I needed to pay the printer?

I went to the banks. They liked what I was doing but politely pointed out that I had no track record. I thought about this response and realized that these bankers had never heard of me or my company before. I set about to remedy that. I sent small news releases out weekly. My company was bringing out this new magazine or that, expanding its operations into this area or that, hiring this person or that as vice-president of sales (vice-presidents get into print more easily than sales managers), and every other positive thing that could possibly be imagined. I concluded each short release with a paragraph about my position as president and my own credentials.

After three months I approached a new bank. "Yes," the banker said, "I've been reading about you and your company. How can I help?" And in short order I had the line of credit I needed. I was the same. My company was the same. I had merely increased my positive public visibility through the effective use of news releases.

A news release is not a feature story. It tells, in the terse style of straight news stories, the facts of your book and its publication. The best releases will be one page in length. This length is manageable and fits easily into filler space in newspapers. In no case should your release run more than a page and a half unless there is something far more newsworthy involved than the mere fact that you have written and published a book.

The shorter and more concise the news release, the more likely it is to be picked up by newspapers.

Always write your release in newspaper style. If you don't, no one will have time to rewrite it, and it will be discarded. If you do not feel that you can copy the style of newspapers you can get a journalist to write one for you. A one-page release will cost upwards of $50, but it may be worth it if this is the only way you can get it done.

News releases must fit available space. This means that editors often lop off a final paragraph or two when they put your release in place. Since you know that this often happens you will get all essential information in the first few lines. The closing, while containing readable information, will be expendable. The release will stand alone with or without them.

A Release for Every Occasion

When should you send out news releases? There are more occasions than you might imagine. Remember that your goal is not only to sell a particular book, but to build your reputation as a poet and literary figure of importance.

Here are some typical occasions that merit news releases:

- You publish a poem in a journal or magazine of note.
- You publish a book. Send a separate release on acceptance and another on publication.
- You are honored at an autograph party.
- You give a talk to a club.
- You give a reading.
- You are elected to an office in an arts organization.
- You start your own publishing company.

How to Get on Television

There are several steps to getting on television. You can succeed, but you may have to throw out several lines to catch a single fish.

- Your first move is to send out a television news release. This varies somewhat from a print media news release, but it conveys the same basic information. Include a routing box on your television news release as follows:

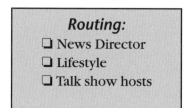

> ### Routing:
> ❏ News Director
> ❏ Lifestyle
> ❏ Talk show hosts

- Double and triple up on your television contacts. Your news release should be beefed up with your complete media kit, sent to talk show hosts by name, and reinforced by personal telephone calls to the same individuals.
- Send out "available for interview" sheets to talk show hosts. These sheets are designed to tell them, at a glance, why you will be a good interview. This is worth some effort, as it is good business to be seen on local and regional talk shows. These shows are constantly on the lookout for anybody doing anything interesting and you, as a published poet, can fill that bill, so long as you let them know just why what you have to say will be interesting. This sheet will include your

photo in the upper right-hand corner, your brief bio, a section telling what your book is about, and, most important, a section suggesting strong viewer-pulling topics, i.e., "How to unlock the creative force within."

- Give them the double whammy. Call them directly *and* send them an available for interview sheet.
- A tip: no-shows are a constant problem on local talk shows. When you speak to the talk show host let them know that you are available on short notice and can fill in for last minute cancellations—a sure way to get your good-looking profile on camera in short order.

How to Prepare for a Television Interview

If you will follow through on these suggestions, you are certainly going to get on the air. The next step is to prepare carefully for your interview. These do not last long: five minutes is the usual, sometimes stretching to ten if commercial time is not filled or if a later guest fails to show up. What will you talk about? Think carefully about this and develop some material that will be as broadly interesting as you can make it.

- Type five or six of the most interesting and leading questions you can think of on an index card. Give this card to the person who is going to interview you. This person will seldom have read your book and will be grateful for your help in making the interview go well.
- Try to come up with questions that will capture the attention of your viewers. "They say that everybody has a book or a poem inside them just waiting to get out. How do you open the creative doors?" and "What advice do you have for aspiring poets?" might be two good ones.
- You might also plant a question about a specific poem that you think will be of interest to your viewers. You will doubtless come up with some great ideas that grow out of your own work and interests.
- Remember that, when it comes to our craft, you are the expert.

There is a web site that talk show hosts and journalists across the country use to prospect for guests. The URL is www.guestfinder.com. There is a charge to register your name, but if there is anything really unique or newsworthy about your book, this site can bring you some welcome media exposure.

RECOMMENDED RESOURCE

Project an air of confidence and authority. Remember my earlier advice on the perils of self-deprecation. There is certainly no place for it on television. Too much untimely modesty can make for a poor interview.

- Always let your viewers know what your book title is and what it is about. Let them know where it can be bought. When you go on the air, make arrangements for a local bookstore to have some copies on hand. Some listeners will undoubtedly go out and buy a copy.

- Television is a visual medium. Be careful with your appearance. Study the show that you are going on. Do the guests sit in chairs? Behind desks? Practice your posture and bearing.

- Bring along an art board that displays the cover of your book or one or two of your poems neatly spray-mounted in place and perhaps bordered. Give this to the director of the show beforehand. They may ask the host to hold up a copy, but they may also use your art board as a lead-in or lead-out.

- Do not neglect radio talk shows. These shows have a tremendous popularity today. I never fail to get calls and inquiries whenever I appear on one of them. Often you will have as much as thirty minutes of time to talk about your work, the writing life, etc.

- After your appearance, the phones may ring. Many listeners and viewers will have missed the part where you tell them how to get hold of your book. Leave a "for further information" card with the show's host and with the station's switchboard operator. On the card, write your name and address, the

Your "Available for Interview" form will give some hard information and tell why you will be an interesting and entertaining guest. It will include your photograph, credentials, and a listing of topics you are prepared to talk about, expressed in the strongest, most viewer-centered language you can come up with. Here, in abbreviated form, is an <u>Available for Interview</u> form that I might invent for this book on publishing poetry. My thanks to writer Peggy Glenn, whose book <u>Publicity for Books and Authors</u> I have quoted elsewhere, for suggesting this marketing idea.

AVAILABLE FOR INTERVIEW

Your photo here

Tom Williams, Ph.D., noted author, editor and publisher. Author of the bestselling book, *Poet Power: The First Ever Marketing Manual and Success Guide for Poets.* Williams is the author of other books such as *Tales of the Tobacco Country,* a collection of history and folklore, *How to Make $100,000 a Year in Desktop Publishing,* and *Breaking Free: How to Win Financial Freedom Through Your Home-based Business.* He is President of Venture Press, a book publishing company based in Washington, NC, and former editor and publisher of *Tar Heel: The Magazine of North Carolina.*

Thousands of everyday people are starved for creative expression. Dr. Williams' ideas and encouragement tell them how to release this creative power in their own lives. On your show, Dr. Williams will talk about such topics as:

- How to unlock the hidden wells of creativity within.
- How to find and explore your secret *idea-center.*
- Nine secrets of publishable poetry.
- How to find hundreds of little-known magazines that will publish your poems.
- How to write, publish, and sell a book of your own poems.

Tom Williams will be available in your area on: _____

CONTACT: Dr. Tom Williams, Address, etc.

title of your book, and details on how and where to buy a copy of it. Alert bookstores to the possible increased demand.

Announce Your Book to Relatives, Friends, and Acquaintances

When you are marketing a book of poetry, every sale counts. Three to five hundred transactions can dispose of an entire first edition. It does not take too many of them, therefore, to make your book a rousing success.

One often overlooked market is that of family and friends. Utilize your Christmas card list, for instance, or your child's wedding announcement list. Under the publisher's name (even if you are your own publisher) send an announcement of publication in a social invitation size envelope. The card inside will bear the message that "Orpheus Publications has the honor to announce the publication of (your title) by (your name)." Then give the date of publication. In the same envelope is another card with the publisher's address on one side and a place for a stamp. On the other side is an order blank. Be sure to state that the copies sent in response to the order will be copies of the first edition and that they will be signed by the author. Include the price, of course. You can generate additional sales by providing space for the names and addresses of those to whom gift copies can be sent, should the buyer wish to order them. Since you do not want to be in the business of billing your friends for books they have bought, indicate that a check for the purchase (with $1 additional for postage) should be included with the reply card.

You may wish to delay sending this announcement for friends whom you expect to invite to your first big marketing gala, your publication autograph party.

This short news release announces the publication of the poet's book. It is concise and easy for the editor to use. Type the words "LOCAL ANGLE" on the front of the envelope to alert the editor that the release concerns someone or something of interest to his immediate community.

John Doe
(919) 999-9999
111 South Muse Place
Artsville, NC 12345

FOR IMMEDIATE RELEASE

Artsville Poet Honored

Artsville poet John Doe has been named winner of the North Carolina Society of Poetry award for best poem on a North Carolina theme for 1991.

In making the award, Marvin Major, President of the society, singled out Doe's "deep understanding of the values that we all cherish: home, family, and community."

Doe's verse has previously appeared in national and regional publications. He is also author of the recently published book, Scenes of the Outer Banks. *Doe is a member of the Artsville Council for the Arts, and Secretary of the creative writing division of the North Carolina Literature Coalition.*

End.

Note to the editor: The enclosed poem may be reproduced "by permission of John Doe. Copyright by John Doe, 2000." Review copies of Scenes of the Outer Banks *may be obtained by calling the telephone number at the top of this release. John Doe is available for interview on topics of literary and artistic interest to the community.*

A news release in the form of a feature story might begin like this. It would be sent to a newspaper—especially smaller papers or weeklies—along with an interesting photo of the author. Always include two or three poems with permission to reprint, and include quotes from poems in the text of the review itself. Don't forget to include ordering info for those who would like to obtain a copy.

Venture Press   *For further Information:*
12445 NW 10 Court   *Tom Williams*
Coral Springs, FL 33071   *(954) 796-0104*

FOR IMMEDIATE RELEASE

New Book Captures People, Places and Spirit
of Historic Washington

"When I first came to the town of Washington, I just knew I had to write about it", says poet Jane Doe of her new book, Visions of Washington. *"It all fascinated me—the river and the marshes, the fishermen in the early morning fog, the rich heritage and history, and especially the people. There is a sense of place here, of roots, that seems so often to be missing these days. I found so much here in this little seacoast town."*

*Doe's book, her third, was published early this month by Venture Press. "We believe it is one of the best we have done in some time," says publisher Tom Williams. "*Visions of Washington will *be a serious contender for the J. J. Jones Medal, awarded by the Literary Society to the best book of poetry by a North Carolinian."*

Many of Visions' *poems profile individuals Doe came to know and admire during her year-long stay. Here, for instance, is Calvin Cullers, tending his nets in the dim light of a river dawn . . . (the article continues with quotes and commentary).*

End.

Send out a release similar to this eight to ten days before any reading or other appearance you may make. Bookstores will advertise you in their shops, but will not give wide circulation to your reading. TV interviews, speeches, awards, etc., should also be announced with a release.

For further information:
John Doe
111 South Muse Place
Artsville, NC 12345
(919) 999-4321

FOR IMMEDIATE RELEASE

Local Writer Will Appear

Artsville poet John Doe will appear on the WXYZ-TV show, "The State of the Arts," this Sunday afternoon at 3:30. The show is hosted by Magnus Magnason, and features people and personalities in the Tri-City arts community.

Doe's recent book, Scenes of the Outer Banks *(Venture Press, 2001), has been widely and positively reviewed. Doe also is the recipient of this year's North Carolina Poetry Society award for best poem on a North Carolina theme.*

Doe is a member of the Artsville Council on the Arts, and Secretary of the North Carolina Coalition for Literature. He is currently a consultant in creative writing to the Artsville School System.

Doe is currently at work on a new book, Southern Porches, *which will be published next year.*

End.

Chapter Ten / The Joys of Signing and Selling: How to Sell Books at Autograph and Publication Parties

Your book is out. News releases have generated stories in your local newspaper and, with any luck, you have appeared in an interview slot on your local morning talk show. The time is ripe for a publication and autograph party. This event has a threefold purpose: it is an important PR and marketing event to promote your present and future work, it is an important opportunity to sell a sizeable number of books, and it is a personal celebration.

Too often, we are content to focus on the last of these reasons, as though a publication party were something that we merely attended as guest of honor, ready to soak up the praise of our families and friends. This is a great mistake. Such an event is not something that someone does to you and for you while you linger humbly in the background until the time comes to have the roses thrown your way. No, a very carefully planned and orchestrated publication party should achieve at least three important goals:

1. Focus attention on you and your work and thus enhance your reputation and public visibility. To seek this visibility is not immodest, unworthy, or un-poetlike. It is, instead, your very stock-in-trade, the thing that will broaden your circle of influence and activity and win more and more readers for your work. Poets live on grants, awards, appointments, fellowships, readings, and presentations. It is your public visibility and reputation that will make these things possible for you. When writers of equal merit are in the running for a grant, the one whose name is most widely known has a decided advantage.

2. Sell enough of your books to recoup publication costs. If your book is a chapbook or printed in a limited edition, this is not an unrealistic goal. A chapbook can be published for, say, $3.00. If you sell the book for $8.95, thirty-five guests who purchase an autographed copy can take you over the top.

3. Experience the deserved pleasure of having your book published and available to others.

To accomplish these goals, your autograph party must be as carefully planned and controlled an event as any you have ever been associated with. There is no room for the amateurish or the tentative.

You Can't Leave It Up to Someone Else

The marketing of an artistic reputation or product (your book) requires all the basic knowhow that you have been absorbing from this book. Though you will be grateful to friends who offer to give a party for you, it is unlikely that any of them, unassisted, will possess the necessary skills to stage an effective marketing event.

This means that no matter who serves as the official host or hostess—whether an individual or a group—you will have to take charge of the arrangements and see that it is all done right. The autograph party has to be scheduled at the right time, the right people have to be invited, the evening planned so as to reach a climax when you want it to, and the purchase of your books made to seem as natural and inevitable as breathing.

You will begin planning your autograph party far in advance, even before the initial publication publicity appears. Nor is it necessary that you have only one of them. You may be able to arrange several in a larger town, or one in the town where you work and another in your home town. But the first of them will be the major one, the one that serves as a kickoff celebration for your new life as a published poet.

Who Will Sponsor Your Party?

Your publication/autograph party may be hosted by an individual or by a group. It may be given by:

- *An arts council or society.* This is a natural choice, if such a body exists in your town and is amenable to sponsoring the event. If you have been an active member, this will facilitate things. Such activities are always investments in your future.
- Sometimes, the arts council itself will not sponsor the event, but will make its premises available to the publisher or to some other individual or group that wishes to do so. This adds a certain stamp of approval and unspoken endorsement to the event and to the quality of your book.
- *A poetry society.* In larger metropolitan areas there is often a privately endowed "poetry society" devoted to encouraging the work of local writers. Such a group may be willing to sponsor your party, especially if you have been active in its work.
- *A writers' club.* Many writers' clubs, though made of prose writers and poets, will still sponsor publication parties for their own members.
- *Your publisher*, as main sponsor or, better, as co-sponsor. Even if you have published the book yourself, there is still the publishing company name you have chosen on the bottom of the title page. In this case, invitations to your party can and should be issued in the name of the publisher.
- *A friend.* A friend may offer to give a party for you. This may be your "official" publication party, or it can be something as simple as a reception in your honor, given in addition to the main event. Even at a reception, your books will be available and your three goals remain unchanged.

Key Questions

When someone expresses an interest in giving an autograph party for you, ask yourself if this person is capable of putting together the event with your help (make sure that they will accept your help). Ask yourself the following questions:

- Do they have the space?
- Do they have the social clout?
- If an organization, does it have an active membership?

The Invitations Themselves

The invitations will be typeset and printed in a standard formal invitation format. This can be done inexpensively at most quick-copy shops that also feature desktop publishing typesetting. An invitation that I have used frequently and successfully reads as follows:

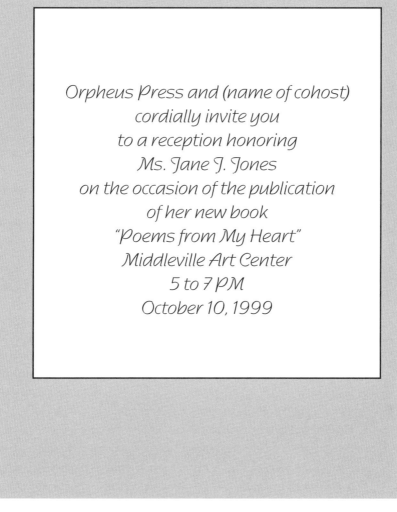

Orpheus Press and (name of cohost)
cordially invite you
to a reception honoring
Ms. Jane J. Jones
on the occasion of the publication
of her new book
"Poems from My Heart"
Middleville Art Center
5 to 7 PM
October 10, 1999

- Are they willing, with your help, to send out large numbers of invitations?
- Can they schedule the autograph party at a time of day most conducive to the best attendance?

You need positive answers to most of these questions, if possible. If your sponsor does not check out against these success criteria, go ahead, but be prepared to do even more of the work yourself. If the person who makes the offer is a good friend, but not right for the big party, suggest a reception instead.

The Guest List

You will send invitations to the most extensive guest list possible. To do this, do not hesitate to offer to help with the costs of printing invitations or postage, if you believe that this will facilitate things.

Your host (or host organization) will undoubtedly rely on you to provide names and addresses of those whom you wish to invite. You should include the following persons on your list:

- Your own family, friends, and acquaintances. These are essentially people who, though they may not be interested in poetry, are surely interested in you and who will come to be a part of the celebration.
- Members of the local arts council.
- Members of any local writers' clubs to which you belong.
- Media representatives and contacts.
- Library and bookstore people, especially independent booksellers.
- Other published writers and would-be writers of your acquaintance.
- Town dignitaries and politicos of note.
- Business associates and others with whom you do business, particularly those for whom you are an important customer. The printer, typesetter, artists, etc., from whom you bought services in getting your book out are prime candidates. Don't

On Success in the Business of Literature

We are social animals and we create ourselves in the eyes of others. The gaze of others defines us, socially and professionally speaking. We must take reasonable care that others see us and think about us as we would wish to be seen and thought about. This means that others need to see us as writers and poets.

forget your lawyer, accountant, physician, and other professionals who count you as a customer.

Be sure to cross-reference these lists to eliminate duplicates. Also eliminate names of individuals who, for one reason or another, you just don't want to show up at the affair. The names you have left will constitute your basic invitation list.

Invitations will be mailed out approximately two weeks in advance. This is not the kind of event anyone is likely to postpone a vacation trip for, so you want the invitation to arrive close enough to the date of the event to be easily remembered.

Regrets only are solicited so that those who might have forgotten to respond to an RSVP will feel free to stop by for congratulations and a glass of wine or a cocktail.

The News Release

You will send a news release to the social editor and to the book editor (if any) of your local newspaper telling of the upcoming event. Your goal is to get it reported as a social event of importance just a few days before the party itself—preferably on the preceding Sunday. This article will serve to remind those who received invitations of the time and place of the event, and it will serve to enhance the event and increase attendance.

The Best Time of Day

What is the best time for your autograph party? Well, you want both husband and wife to attend, if possible. You don't want to conflict with more (to the guest) important social commitments. You want to fit in easily with personal schedules.

I have found that an event scheduled from five until seven or seven-thirty, on a weekday night, works best. Of the available weekdays, experience shows that Tuesday and Thursday work best. The time slot is easily manageable. Business persons can stop by on the way home from work, dressed in their business clothes. Wives and husbands can easily meet at the party location. And the time commitment is lim-

Names and Addresses Are Valuable

One thing you want to be very careful to do is to note the name and address of every person who buys your book or comes to a reading. You can do this very easily and naturally by asking for their name and address at the time of the purchase or by asking attendees at a reading to fill out an "information sheet." This list, added to the one you used to send out invitations to your autograph party, constitutes your own mailing list of persons interested in you and your books. It will grow and grow as you appear more and more frequently in public. Whenever you bring out a new book, you will send a pre-publication notice and special offer on an autographed first edition to those whose names are on your list. You will also use it to recruit people for workshops or seminars that you may give or any consulting services that you may, in time, wish to offer to less experienced, less market-wise poets.

ited enough to assure anyone that the event, though pleasant enough, is not likely to monopolize their evening. Correctly organized, however, and with a good mix of guests, autograph parties have a way of becoming more enjoyable than most imagined they would be, and guests linger longer (and buy more books) than they expected to.

The Best Location

While a friend who is sponsoring your party may be quite willing to have it in her home, this may not be the best choice. A public place, preferably arts-related, works better than a private residence.

I think this is true because individuals who simply want to drop in can do so more easily when the autograph party is taking place in a public place. They do not feel as obliged to go home from work, shower, and change as they would if attending a cocktail party in someone's home. Attendance will be larger. Such a location, too, helps focus attention on you as poet and allays any reservations an individual might have about the promotional aspects of the evening. In the absence of other available locations, however, a quite successful evening can be planned at a home.

What kind of public place? I recommend that arrangements be made to have the event in the reception area, say, of the local museum of art or in the facilities of the local arts council. In your area other such locations may be possible. You may also consider renting space, if it is affordable, in a local hotel or motel, but I would do this only if nothing else was available and if the space itself was often used by the community for receptions and similar events.

Keep the area as small as you can relative to the number of people you expect to serve. (No more than 50% of those invited, in all likelihood, will attend.) It is far better to have more people in a smaller space than the same number of guests lost in the expanse of a ballroom.

The Physical Arrangements

Do not spread out over too large an area. Provide a table of attractive but affordable *hors d'oeuvres* somewhere near the center of the area where you wish the bulk of the guests to congregate. The kind you can buy ready-made at many grocery store delicatessen departments or even at wholesale houses like Sam's Club or Costco are perfectly suitable. To one side you will position a table where someone will serve white wine or perhaps simple cocktails, depending on your personal tastes and budget. But it is important to have one or the other of these beverages. Punch will be available for the nondrinkers.

Not too distant from the food and drink—but far enough away to be perceived as a separate center of attention—will be a table on which your books are stacked, along with a poster board and easel with an enlargement of the cover, quotes from reviewers, and perhaps a "Congratulations" banner of some kind. This table will be the center of book sales as the reception progresses. Someone will be present at this table at all times to handle the money, make change, etc. You do not want to do this yourself. The sales table should be positioned so that guests leaving the party will be aware of its presence, since they will have to pass close by.

Another small table will be set up with a single chair. At this table you will sign books purchased by the guests and brought to you. Most writers sign on the title page, near the place where their name is printed. Ask for whom the book is being bought, and be sure to check the spelling of unfamiliar names. You can sign simply, "Best wishes to . . . ," followed by your name and the date.

Signing and Selling

At about six or six fifteen (if you started up at five) the crowd will peak before starting to thin out a little. At this moment the host will get the attention of the crowd, welcome the guests and thank them for coming, tell about you and your book (using information you have provided), and offer a toast. You will respond, briefly. Your host will then announce that you will be available to autograph this *first edition* (this phrase has strong sell-power) of your books as they are brought to you. Then she bids the guests to continue the celebration.

At this point you have to let the guests know what to do. For most, if not all of them, this will be the first autograph party they have been to. *They will not know what is expected of them. You will have to show them by example.* Arrange for several friends to purchase copies (real purchases or not) at this time. They need to pull out the bucks and get change so that others will know what is to be done. Then they will take their books to you for signing. After the signing they will proudly show their copy off to other guests at the party.

All this can be done quite naturally, and it is absolutely essential to initiate the process of getting book sales going.

Bookstore Parties

Occasionally you see an ad for a bookstore autograph signing. An author will be present to sign copies of books bought there by customers. These sometimes work, at the right place and time, and with a very well-known author. But they are a great gamble, and usually fail to attract the crowds that you need to be successful.

Nobody is free to go by the store during business hours, and, in the late afternoon, when all the world is at home enjoying an end-of-the-day cocktail, who wants to go to a shopping mall to watch some poet sign a book? And there's nothing lonelier than an autograph party to which no one comes.

Don't depend on bookstore autograph parties alone unless you are very well-known in the community and unless the community is a very unusual one in its support of literature and the arts. I might try it in a bookstore on Harvard Square or in downtown Chapel Hill, but unless I was supported by a folk singer, a band, and a group of ethnic dancers, I would not count on success even then.

Chapter Eleven / How to Sell Your Books at Poetry Readings

Make no mistake about it, ninety-five percent of all books of poetry are sold at poetry readings, and that is where you will sell most of yours. And because they are so important, poetry readings are—or should be—full-scale, carefully planned performances of which you and your poems are the stars. Unfortunately, these powerful marketing events are often poorly planned or not planned at all, and that is a great waste.

At a reading, you have everything going for you. The audience is always friendly and well-disposed toward you. They have, after all, chosen to come to this place to meet you and listen to you read your own work. Some are poets themselves, some are lovers of poetry, and some are friends who have come along to show their support for you. All are positive listeners. They are here because they want to talk poetry, hear poetry, think poetry, meet at least one successful poet (you), and exchange ideas about their craft. They will gather any crumbs of gratification (usually all they will get at most readings) offered to them and leave very grateful for having gotten anything at all.

Your audience deserves a good show and you, as author of the poems being read, certainly deserve one. More than that, *you need it. But unless you take charge and make it happen, neither you nor your audience is likely to enjoy the occasion.* For the sad fact is that poetry readings can be deadly dull. This is quite a paradox. A poet uses language to achieve the most intense communication possible, and yet the evening's readings are all too often devoid of any life at all, let alone passion.

Something Different

The challenge is to make your own readings something different, something above and beyond the ordinary. Think of a favorite play.

135

When inexperienced people sit around in a circle and read the text in low-key voices, the sparks do not fly, the tinder does not catch and the fire does not begin to burn. But let fine actors utter those same words in the context of a production and the heart begins to race. Something important is happening, and the spectators are caught up in it.

An Art That Can Be Learned

You need to convert your readings, insofar as you can, into a performance that will catch your listeners in the same way. Most of us are not natural performers. Fortunately, putting on a dramatic reading is an art that can be learned. As you work at developing your reading and as you do more of them you will become more and more adept at achieving the kind of powerful communication you want. Your poetry is art. But your reading of it is—must be—*showbiz.*

Molding Audience Expectations

The psychologists talk about "mind-set." They use these words to refer to the mental and emotional *expectation* in individuals and groups that predisposes them to react to what they see and hear in a particular way. This is one of the great secrets of show business. Everything about a successful performance, all the peripherals and props, must predispose the audience to think "This is great!" And if that is what they do think, they are predisposed to enjoy, to approve, to applaud.

A typical rock music concert provides a wonderful example. What is the reality of it? Rather unattractive young performers stalk about the stage with unpleasant expressions on their faces, shouting bad lyrics to worse music. The music itself is performed with mediocre skill by musicians of more energy than talent. Yet thousands of spectators stand, cheer, and generally carry on as though in utter ecstasy of artistic enjoyment. They *experienced what they expected to experience.*

The Packaging Makes the Product

With rare exceptions, it is the packaging rather than the product that provokes this frenzied response. The mind-set of the audience is carefully prepared to facilitate it.

At such concerts there are only five or six musicians and singers

performing on the stage. Yet the day before, legions of lighting special-
ists, sound technicians, stage hands, and others arrived with truckloads
of paraphernalia and props—enough to make the magic appearance
of the Wizard of Oz look like a child's sparkler by comparison. Smoke
rises from the stage, electronic fireworks illuminate vast auditoriums,
sound systems capable of deafening a major modern city amplify beyond all imagining the lead singer's clumsiest stroking of his guitar.
The excitement is palpable. It is not just a concert; it is an *experience.*

Well, of course, you may not be able—or even willing—to match
that act. But you can and must learn from it. Always keep in mind that
the atmosphere of your reading is as important as the reading itself. If
you want your audience to listen to you and to react enthusiastically to
your verse (and buy your book), you've got to work to create an envi-
ronment that encourages them to do so.

The fact is that most people don't know what to do at a poetry
reading including, in most cases, the poet. At a basketball game, when
a player makes an unbelievably deft move and scores a key basket, you
stand up and cheer. But when a poet turns out a near perfect line or
passes through one of those "sudden rightnesses" that great poetry is
made of, what's to do? Shout "Yeah!" as they do at jazz concerts? Ex-
actly. That is precisely the kind of reaction one should encourage. Yet
the atmosphere of most readings is more like that of afternoon tea at
the Ladies' Missionary Society. Any show of real emotion is out of place.
The atmosphere is not one of freedom but of inhibition.

You Can Change All That

You've got to work to change that. It may be a tall order, but you
can do it. As you do more and more readings—of your own poetry and
perhaps even the poetry of others—you will get better and better at it
and have more and more fun. Those who come will truly enjoy themselves, and will create a reputation and positive public visibility for you
that will be an asset for years to come. How are you going to do all this?
Here are some steps that will get you started along the way.

Be Aggressive in Lining Up Readings

Line up as many readings as you can. In the beginning, explore every possibility, no matter how modest the opportunity. The first few readings are like a shakedown cruise. You get everything running right and coordinated. You learn your performer's craft.

In order to accomplish this, you will want to do the following things:

- Utilize the same media kit that you used for your newspaper and TV publicity in building a schedule of readings. Send it to program chairpersons, then follow up with a telephone call. In each news article about your activities and in each TV appearance, get the word out that you do readings.

- Approach writers' clubs, arts councils, public schools, community colleges, junior colleges, four-year colleges and universities, and other special organizations whose interests may coincide with the themes in your poetry. If your poetry is religious in nature, for instance, church groups may be interested in having you. Let those responsible for program planning know that you are ready, willing, and able to put on a superior performance at a moment's notice.

- Stress the fact that your readings go beyond the ordinary and create enthusiastic audience response and active audience participation. *Let them know that, more than a simple reading, your appearance will be an educational experience, a performance.*

- Treat each of these readings with all the care and professionalism that you can muster.

Take Charge

There are sayings that have been around for years. They have been around and are still around because they are very, very true. One is that "If you want something done right you have to do it yourself." Another comes from management seminars on small business. "Nobody," this saying goes, "cares about your business the way you do."

You will do well to take both these pieces of advice to heart. As soon as you have a reading lined up, get in touch with the program chairperson. Find out who is responsible for getting the space ready for your appearance. Write up a paragraph or two outlining your needs, props, etc., for the chairperson's use. Offer your help in arranging things the way you want them.

Create Powerful Publicity

One of the most important parts of taking charge is to make sure that publicity plans are well-made, well-scheduled, and as effective as possible. Here are some items to think about:

- Remember that your program chairperson knows very little about publicizing an event beyond, maybe, putting a little note in an organization newsletter.
- If there is to be such a note, you write it for your program chairperson. Fill it with the kind of information that will attract more attendees. Build excitement and anticipation. Let people know that your reading will be something out of the ordinary and is not to be missed.
- Send news releases announcing your appearance (and afterward, releases telling about it) to the local newspaper and to local radio and television stations.
- Offer to appear on their shows with some teasers from your performance.
- If possible organize a telephone campaign to contact people who might be interested in coming.
- Contact English teachers and ask that your program be announced in class. Perhaps it could be made the subject of a theme or paper.
- If the organization's budget—or your own budget—can stand it, send out invitations to a selected guest list.

Nothing happens by itself. You have to make things happen. Remember that no one is as interested in your success as you are. What is your program chairperson's chief concern? That the program not bomb. Convince the chairperson that you simply will not stand for anything less than a smashing success and that the glory will be his or hers as well as yours.

Create a Usable Space

Visit the premises several days before your performance. Allow yourself plenty of time to set things up (arrange the stage!) to suit you. Make certain that the room itself has a warm feeling and is as conducive to direct communication as possible. Often you may scout around the building and suggest that another location might be much more effective for your presentation. Decide where you want the lectern located, where the easels and other props go, where the refreshment table is to be located, and where your table of books for autographing will be.

You do not want too few people to rattle around in a large space. You don't want to be cramped, but it is better to come close to filling up your space than to have yawning gaps of emptiness to fill up with your energy. Water boils faster in a small container; the steam whistles more quickly from a small teapot. The same dynamic relationship between space and energy holds true between performers and the space they work in. Test the PA system that you will be using.

Remember That You Are Planning a Performance

Plan your evening as though you were planning a performance—which is just what you *are* doing. Good performances are well-organized performances. Don't wing it. Don't trust to luck and improvise as you go. Have the presentation well-planned. Develop specific answers to questions such as these:

- When do I arrive?
- What am I going to say as I mingle with the audience during the social hour that will set the stage for my reading?
- Who will introduce me?
- What should the introducer say about me as a good lead in?
- Which pieces will I read, and in what order, so that I build to a climax?
- How do I get the audience involved?
- What do I say in closing?
- How do I let the audience know in the most effective way that I will be available to autograph my books?

Every good dramatic performance, as Aristotle taught two thousand years ago, has a beginning, a middle, and an end. It builds slowly, reaches a climax, and then comes to a strong and satisfactory conclusion. Your reading must do the same thing.

Call On Friendly (and Free) Consultants in Staging and Drama

The one-man show has had a strong run of success on the stage in recent years: Hal Holbrook as Mark Twain and James Whitmore as Harry Truman are two examples that come to mind.

What makes such shows successful? Find out, and utilize these techniques yourself. If you have a friend in a community theater or an acquaintance who has experience in stage direction, consult them. If you don't know such people, perhaps you can find them. Go to the local arts council, community college, or even the high school English department. Odds are you can find people who are ready and willing to help with suggestions and ideas. The question you put to your informal consultants is straightforward: How can I make a poetry reading a dramatic success? Gather as many ideas as you can, collate and sort them, and use the ones that work best for you.

Every Detail Is Important

Everything is important: what you wear, how you look, your tone of voice and the way you project it, the clarity of your diction and the expressiveness with which you read. Some rehearsal is definitely called for. Check your presentation on video. Your expert-friend-consultant can furnish important feedback here.

Before the Reading

You will have taken care that the room is completely set up according to your instructions before the audience arrives. If necessary, you will do this yourself. Here are some tips:

- The refreshment table will be in place. Refreshments will be served both before and after the reading.

- Your autograph table is nearby, with stacks of books and display boards (as described above for autograph parties).
- As people begin to come in, mingle with them and introduce yourself. Ask about their work and their interests, and listen attentively. Have someone nearby who can spot key attendees and point them out to you, introducing you to those whom you do not know.
- Do not socialize too long at this time. Allow the crowd to assemble, have a glass of wine, and shake your hand.
- Then you wind your way to the front of the room where you are to do your reading. No later than five minutes after the announced time for the beginning, you begin.

As the Evening Begins

There are some important preliminaries to attend to before the reading proper begins.

- An introduction must be carefully done—so carefully, in fact, that you can't just leave it up to the program chairperson, who probably has no idea how to go about it. You will write an introductory script and give it to the chairperson. It can then be read or, if the chairperson is at ease in front of an audience, paraphrased.
- You must let the audience know what the overall organization of the evening will be—that you will give your reading and that afterwards refreshments will be served. During that time, you will hope to meet with everyone present and answer all questions and "just have fun talking about writing and publishing poetry."
- The introducer will also announce that you will be available to autograph your books.
- The introducer (or you) will let the audience know who you are and what you have written. If you have published widely, mention some of the more impressive publications. If there are reviews, the introducer can quote these, so long as it is

done in good spirits and in a low key. Many of those present will be poets (in fact or in their dreams) and will enjoy hearing about your professional trials, tribulations, and triumphs, so long as this is done in the right spirit of fun.

Down with Victorian Restraint!

Let the audience know that this is going to be a reading unlike others that they may have attended. Let them know that you welcome interaction, questions, even interruptions. Let them know that it is OK to make noise, to clap, whistle, shout encouragement—that it is OK to have fun with poetry.

I have often been struck by the fact that at poetry readings there seems to be no socially acceptable audience reaction other than polite, Victorian restraint. The poet finishes reading a piece and is met by dead silence. He has no idea where he stands with the audience. If they like it, silence. If they don't like it, silence. If they don't understand it, silence. And on to the next page. It is only their love of poetry that keeps them (mostly) awake.

This just won't do. I have often—and very seriously—thought of giving out Halloween noisemakers at the door. As stirring passages are read appropriate sounds of approval can be made by shaking, swinging, whirling, or blowing into the devices furnished to the audience. Certainly it would impress on those attending that I was serious in inviting their reaction. It could work very nicely.

Warm Them Up

When you watch a live show on television—a comedy show like the *Tonight Show* or even a quiz show—the host always walks out to thunderous applause as the show begins. How, you may ask, could a cold audience reach such a pitch of enthusiasm in so short a time? The answer is that the audience is not cold at all. For an hour or more it has been warmed up, carefully primed for the moment you have just witnessed.

How can you warm your audience up? Here are some random ideas that will illustrate the kind of thing that I am talking about. These fit my personality. Others will occur to you that fit yours.

- Kick things off in a light vein, establishing a tone of fun and relaxed interplay for the evening. You might try something like a humorous introduction to the kinds of silence that universally befall poets at their readings. Then you may suggest what you think can be done about it and lead the audience in practicing boos and cheers and in using their noisemakers.
- Read surefire zingers from other poets—parts of Whitman's *Song of Myself*, for instance. Such poetry can be fairly shouted out at an audience and ought to be greeted with shouts of approval and choruses of "Right-on's." Lead the cheers yourself. Also include some dismal stuff that you can all hiss and boo.
- Then read other well-known poems to indicate the range of reaction possible. Read difficult poems. Read them first as though you assume everyone understands. Then hand out a sheet with the poem printed on it and read again. Stress that poems are made with words, rhythms, and sounds, but also with the semantic properties of those sounds. So we may get more from it when we follow the text, at least the first time, with our eyes, especially when the poem is dense or difficult.
- Ask questions of your audience. Point at them. Jump up and down and yell at them if necessary, but get them involved.

Develop Your Own Patter

A stand-up performer continually talks to the audience, whetting its appetite, building its interest, heightening its reaction to the next part of the act.

When I was a boy I loved to go down to the stage shows that they used to put on at the old Bijou theatre in downtown Savannah. My favorites were the performances of the sleight-of-hand magicians. These old-time troupers would stand alone on the stage, perhaps with the help of a single assistant, sometimes with no help at all. They would surround the act of magic with constant talk. They would tell in all seriousness how they discovered the next marvel in the mysterious east. They would make us keenly aware of the difficulties of accomplishing a particularly complicated feat, such that we appreciated it all the more when it actually happened. They would entertain and amuse us with anecdotes and stories as the evening wore on.

A poet is a magician, too—a magician of words—and effective patter is just as necessary to his own act as to any other. What kind of patter? You will discover bits and pieces of it as you gain experience. For instance:

- Introduce each poem fully.
- Tell stories that let the audience see you as a human being struggling to find expression for a feeling, emotion, or experience that is particularly important to you.
- Tell them about the technical problems you encountered and how you solved them.
- You may find it useful to provide copies of any difficult pieces you are going to read or of any that you are going to use as examples in your talk.
- Understand that when you skip this patter and proceed to read your poems without the necessary introduction they are over before the audience has even begun to focus its attention on the piece you are reading. You lose the audience before you begin. The reading of a lyric poem is a little like the Kentucky Derby. The race itself is over in a matter of minutes. It's the preliminaries that make the Derby the event that it is.
- Sprinkle your presentation with talk of other poets that you know and their own challenges and triumphs.
- Tell humorous—or otherwise—stories of how you got started and how you published your first bit of verse in that grade school newspaper.
- The more personal and direct your patter, the more warmly involved your listeners become and the more effective your reading will be.

As you do more and more readings, your patter will become more and more effective. You try new things, keep the ones that work best and discard the others.

Flyers such as this one can easily be created on your desktop computer and put out for distribution two weeks before your reading. In the event that your reading will be at an art center or bookstore, the staff can wear pin-on buttons like the one shown here. They can be produced at Kinko's or similar copy centers for $2 each.

An Evening of Poetry!

Calling all poets and lovers of poetry! Come meet poet Tom Williams. Williams will read from his latest work and talk about the art of poetry and the work of poets today.

- Join in the discussion.
- Take part in the question and answer session.
- Find out about new publishing opportunities for poets.
- Network with fellow poets and writers.
- Enjoy yourself.

Arnold Art Center

February 29th 2002

Poet Fest!

Poet Tom Williams Reads His Work, Talks about the World of Poetry

Arnold Art Center

February 29th 2002

Develop Your Own "Stump Speech"

Politicians who tour the country during electoral campaigns develop what they call a stump speech. Since they obviously cannot prepare a new talk for each of the scores of stops along their way, they develop one presentation that is slightly altered to suit individual groups and circumstances.

The presentation you develop is your poetical stump speech. You do not have to create a new presentation each time you go out. Instead, you keep refining the materials you have developed. Stick with what works best. You might use different anecdotes for grade school, high school, and university audiences, but the overall performance will be the same.

There will come a time when a dangerous illusion begins to form itself in your mind. You have done your routine so often that you will feel that others must have heard it as many times as you have and become bored with it. If this were true, every Broadway play, even the best, would close after the first month.

This is a common but mistaken feeling among those who appear frequently in public. Remember that for each new audience your presentation is as fresh as the dew and that your only challenge is to remain as enthusiastic and involved as they are.

These Techniques Will Work for You

Everything I say in this chapter, all the techniques I recommend, will work. I know this because I have used them all. Most important, however, is the principal of the thing: *a poetry reading must be treated as a performance.*

There are certainly different approaches that will work, and many that may work very well for you when they would not for me or anyone else. These grow out of your special talents and interests. Maybe you will strum on a guitar while you read your verse. Maybe you will appear in costume. Maybe you will get the audience involved in creating an instant poem through games like the surrealists' "Exquisite Corpse" (*Cadavre exquis*), where nouns, verbs, exclamations, etc., are written down by the assembled group on separate scraps of paper and a poem is made by drawing them out of hats as needed. The results can often be extraordinary in their creation of powerful and astonishing imagery.

But whatever you do, your fame and name will spread, and, if you work persistently to schedule readings and then do them with drama and flair, you will begin a gratifying career of writing, publishing and selling your poems. And—wonder of wonders—you may even begin to make money. The fact that you treat your readings as performances will put you in a class apart.

Sell Your Poems

During the reading, you will have created a spirited and pleased group of new friends. When the performance is over, many of them will gather around the "back of the room" table where you have spread out your books to continue the fun, discuss poetry, and stretch the evening as much as possible.

You will, of course, want to sell some books. Again, the path of wisdom is to have a friend make the first purchase to let the others know just how to go about it. The sponsors of the reading can be recruited to make change. You can also do this yourself, but it is difficult to carry on conversations, autograph books and make change at the same time.

You should take steps to optimize your sales and your profits. The attitude that poetry is a genteel activity not to be sullied by mere money is widespread—and it is as strange as it is wrong. Do you not like to eat? Do you not travel, buy books, give presents to the kids at Christmas?

You can offer other books for sale as well as your own. "How-to" titles (like this one, for instance) can be bought from their publishers at discounts ranging from 40 to 50 percent, usually depending on the quantities purchased. The difference between your purchase price and the retail price that you sell them for is all profit.

Talk to your audience about these books. Work some mention of them naturally into your presentation. Describe how and in what ways they have been valuable to you. Hold them up in your hand. You cannot help but sell some of them at each reading. When you are firmly established, you might arrange with your bank to offer charge card service.

You might also offer audio cassettes of your own presentations and the presentations of others, which you will purchase and sell on the same discount terms.

Chapter Twelve / How to Sell Your Books in Bookstores and Other Retail Outlets

Although most books will be sold at readings, autograph parties, and other personal appearances, a significant number can be sold through retail outlets. The most promising of these outlets are, of course, bookstores. But just as important are greeting card shops, gift shops, souvenir shops, specialty shops related to the topic of your book, and even catalogs.

As you read through this chapter, you will see that the choice of a title can be very important indeed, and the marketing implications of your choice should—within reason—be foremost in your mind when you choose one. Are your poems inspirational? Do they celebrate love and fidelity? Places, events? Your womanhood or manhood? Whatever your slant, make it clear in the title. Doing so can open many specialty sales avenues for your book and greatly increase the number of copies that you will sell.

General Bookstores

Bookstores vary widely in size and kind. At the top of the bookstore food chain are the major players like Barnes and Noble, Borders, Books-a-Million, and a few others. These companies sell books through their ever-growing number of so-called "superstores."

Close behind are the major independent (usually locally owned) booksellers. In a university or college town there may be two or three independents, but, in general, times have grown hard for the independents, who often find it difficult to compete with the superstores. In most towns there will be only one locally-owned bookstore that carries a wide selection of stock, and perhaps not even that. The most successful independents, may actually be mini-chains, with two or more stores located within a region or state. Twenty years ago, B. Dalton and Waldenbooks, with their mall locations, were important outlets, but they have now declined to a secondary level of importance. Even so, in towns where they are the only bookstores available, they are usually quite willing to display books by local and regional authors.

Specialty Bookstores

As Barnes and Noble and Borders began to gobble up massive shares of the bookselling market, other booksellers have increasingly taken refuge in specialty bookstores, where, by limiting their selection of titles to a narrow range of subject matter, they can do an even better job than the big boys. Typical specialty bookstores? Here are some examples gleaned from the yellow pages:

- New Age Bookstores.
- Religious Bookstores. These come in all shapes and sizes— Protestant, Roman Catholic, fundamentalist and denominational.
- Gay and Lesbian Bookstores.
- Nautical Bookstores.
- African-American Bookstores.
- Craft Bookstores.
- Children's Bookstores.
- Bookstores for Teachers and Educators (K-12).
- College and University Bookstores.
- Antiquarian Bookstores.
- Hospital Bookstores.
- Airport Bookstores.

If any of these specialty bookstores is right for your book of poetry, you can usually arrange for the store to carry your book on consignment (see below). I typeset and designed a book called *Love, Desire and Understanding*, by Kirkwood Ferguson. The author has now sold out his first edition of 1,000 copies by giving readings in predominantly gay and lesbian bookstores. Meditative, inspirational, and even humorous collections could sell well in hospital bookstores. Books with African-American themes would do well in ethnic-specialized stores. Specialty bookstores can be an important outlet for you.

Researching the Bookstores

Begin by compiling a mailing list of bookstore contacts. For each store you will want an address, telephone number and fax number. You will also want the name of the person who handles special events, such as writers' club meetings, poetry readings and author signings. In small stores, this person will probably be the owner. Larger stores usually assign this duty to a staff member, often called a "community relations" person or a "special events coordinator."

This list will be invaluable to you as you promote your own books and those of others published in your poetry series. (For a discussion on publishing a poetry series, see chapter eight.)

One of the best sources for this kind of information is the web site of the American Booksellers Association (http://www.bookweb.org/infohub/). Most booksellers are members, and their stores will be listed on the association web site by state and city.

The ABA web site gives all the information you will need, including the names of owners. A sample listing, taken directly from the internet, is shown below:

Books & Books, Inc. [Coral Gables, FL]
Address: 265 Aragon Ave.
Country: USA
Phone: (305)442-4408
Fax: (305)444-9751
Email: books296@aol.com
Description: Since opening in 1982, Mitchell Kaplan has encouraged book lovers to browse our extensive collection of fine fiction, art and architectural books, poetry, classics, nonfiction, best sellers, children's books, and cookbooks. Rare and Antiquarian too!

This listing tells you that Books & Books is an independent bookstore with a general collection of titles, leaning toward the literary. The contact person is Mitch Kaplan, the owner. The street address, telephone number, fax number, and email address are all given. The ABA web site includes listings for over four thousand bookstores across the country. You will not, however, find listings for the chains and superstores, which are not members of the association. For these, check the yellow pages of your telephone book, contact the superstores, and ask for the information you need: special events coordinator (by name), fax number, telephone number, and street address.

Borders has a store locator site on the Internet at www. bordersstores.com. When you go to that site you can choose stores by region, state and city. Below is the internet entry for a Borders store a few blocks from my home. There are similar entries for every Borders store in the U.S. By calling the numbers furnished on the site, you can get in touch with the individual you want to talk to:

Borders Books & Music
   700 University Drive, Coral Springs, FL 33071
Books Department
   954.340.3307
   954.344.9833 FAX
Where We Are: On University Drive, northwest corner
   of Atlantic Boulevard near Coral Square Mall.
   Store Hours: Monday-Saturday 9 AM to 11 PM. Sunday
9 AM to 9 PM.

You can also use the yellow pages to locate other non-ABA members and the smaller specialty stores.

Dealing with Bookstores

Face it. You will never get your book of poetry into the bookstores through normal trade distribution channels. Most poets can't find a wholesaler or distributor who will even handle their books, let alone market them to bookstores. The "economic facts of life," as we outlined them earlier in this book, make this inevitable.

Only personal contact will work, one-on-one, poet-to-bookstore. But where this kind of contact is possible, it works very well. Bookstores are hungry for literary events to attract readers and as pegs to hang their PR and advertising efforts on. Even the supermarket-style

One of the best sources of information about independent and specialty bookstores is the web site of the American Booksellers Assn. The URL is http://www.bookweb.org/infohub/. Borders has a store locator site on the internet at www. bordersstores.com.

RECOMMENDED RESOURCE

superstores have their coffee bars and continue to do everything possible to cultivate the image of an authentic literary hangout. And what is more authentically literary than poetry?

Here's how to cash in on this market:

- Put on your marketing hat: As a poet you can be as ethereal, other-worldly and impractical as you wish. But as a marketer of your poems, you have to take on—or at least understand—the duties of a business person. It is true that an individual who does not love books is unlikely to open a bookstore; however, the bookseller pays the rent not by loving books, but by selling them. If the bookseller believes that you can help him do this, you will be welcomed most heartily into the store.

- Be prepared: Show up for your appointment at the bookstore with your ideas and materials organized. Sell yourself, but be succinct. Come across as a writer who can be good for the store and make things happen. Among the materials you should have available are the following:

    1. A personal information flyer that contains a brief bio, a list of other books you have written, if any, a photograph (scanned and printed out on your laser printer is OK), and topics that you intend to (or can) cover in your presentation.
    2. Quotes from testimonials and letters of thanks for readings and presentations given elsewhere.
    3. Copies of printed reviews of your book.
    4. The book itself.

- Create a value-added dimension. Come up with a slant that

will make your reading or presentation stand out from others.

- List other topics you can discuss, perhaps a poet-centered, how-to-get-published discussion that will attract a more people. The how-to features pull much better than a reading alone, especially if your name is still relatively unknown.

- Offer to lead a roundtable discussion of materials and manuals.

- Offer to "hand sell" other books. The bookstore is providing you a forum, along with some PR and advertising. Suggest that the bookstore set up a special table with reference books and manuals related to writing on it. You can pick up and mention these books during the course of your reading or during the question and answer session. Bookstores call this "hand selling," and they love it.

- Offer to host a regular poetry night or "open mike" session. At these, present yourself as leader and mentor and always read some of your own verse, thereby promoting your book.

- Provide promotional aids. Ask what the bookstore would like you to do in the way of publicizing and promoting your appearance. Some ideas that you can suggest:
  1. Invite members of your writers' club.
  2. Post announcements on library bulletin boards.
  3. Write and send news releases to small, neighborhood newspapers, as well as any major daily newspapers that post a list of area readings on their book page.
  4. Provide large, pin-on buttons to salespeople. (See the previous chapter for a sample pin.) These buttons are great for focusing attention on your event.

Discounts and Dollars

Bookstores normally operate on a 40% discount from their wholesalers. All the books that you see on the shelves were acquired this way. If a book retails for $20, the bookstore purchases it for $12. When it sells, the bookstore keeps $8 to cover all overhead and operating expenses and make a profit. While 40% may seem high to you if you are not familiar with the retail business, it is actually a ten percent lower discount than retail merchants in other trades normally get and makes it tough on bookstores to turn a profit.

Normally your books of poetry will be acquired on a strict consignment basis: you will bring them in, give your reading, sell what you can, and divvy up the proceeds with the store. On a one-time consignment basis, you may be able to negotiate a 20-30% discount rather than the standard 40%. If so, that's good. But don't hesitate to pay the full 40% if the bookstore requests it. This is the profit margin they need to stay in business.

On books that you leave at the store to sell, you will negotiate a consignment agreement. Fill out the consignment agreement in duplicate, leaving one copy for the bookstore and keeping one for yourself. A sample consignment agreement is reproduced in this chapter. Note that the agreement specifies the number of copies left, the discount at which the bookstore will acquire the books, and the date when sales are to be checked and reported.

Non-Bookstore Sales

On non-bookstore sales, the system is slightly different.

- When books are left on consignment, the discount is normally 20% to 30%.
- Otherwise, books are purchased outright by the merchant at a discount of 50%, the standard discount for retail, non-bookstore merchants.

Poetry is an impulse purchase. Few of us go to bookstores with the idea of shopping around for a book of verse. If we see one there, and like it, we may buy it. What you have to recognize is that this impulse can strike a potential reader in a wide variety of shopping situations, and you need to get your book in the customer's hands as frequently and often as possible. Consider the following locations:

- *Card shops.* Browsers in a Hallmark shop looking for a special card may be attracted to a small book of verse, attractively packaged, that expresses the message they wish to convey.

- *Florist shops*. People who purchase bouquets for loved ones may be attracted to a small book of verse displayed strategically on a rack near the signature cards.
- *Gift shops*. Shoppers in gift shops may purchase your book to accompany their gift or as the gift itself. Poetry will be perceived as a highly personal and unusual present, even though it is a relatively inexpensive one. What else can your buy for $10 that will mean so much?
- *Tourist and souvenir shops*. Travelers looking for a meaningful souvenir of a place that they have particularly enjoyed will buy a collection of verse, perhaps illustrated with line drawings, devoted to that particular location. I am thinking again of my mythical collection, *Key West Cats*. There are many such opportunities. When I first started out in business, I used to drive around business neighborhoods with a hand-held tape recorder, collecting names of advertising prospects. I always found far more of them than I ever could have imagined before setting out on my marketing safari. Sales ideas popped into my mind by the dozens. The same technique will work for you, too, in your search for outlets for your poetry.
- *Display Aids*. The buyer does not seek out impulse purchases. He sees them, likes them, and, on the spur of the moment, buys them. Sales of poetry work best when your book is displayed at or near the cash register, at the so-called "point-of-purchase."

A friend of mine, poet Alicia Sirkin, recently published a small, 24-page (plus cover) chapbook called *Reflections from the Heart*. Handsomely designed—in spite of its simple, saddle-stitched format—Alicia's book sold over 700 copies during the weeks when it was displayed at the point of purchase in major bookstores. This is quite a satisfactory sale for a chapbook of verse. Most never sell more than two or three hundred copies. However, the book was recently placed on the shelves with other books of poetry, where sales have fallen off markedly. Why? Well, the prospective reader has to pick it up and leaf through it to feel its full appeal. Many did this while waiting at the cash register. Far fewer do it now that it is virtually hidden on the shelves, just one title among many. Alicia is currently developing strategies to get her book back into the limelight.

There are two things that you can do to help draw attention to your book. You can furnish display wire of cardboard racks to display books upright on the checkout counter. A quick Internet search will uncover several sources. Cardboard racks are sturdy and can easily be spruced up with material output on your color printer. And you can provide small, stand-up posters to place beside your book. These can be printed out on a color printer and laminated before being glued to a small easel-type stand. They can be quite attractive.

Catalogs

As I write this chapter, the Christmas shopping season is just getting under way. Every mail delivery brings four or five catalogs of all kinds of gift items. But catalogs are not merely seasonal. They keep coming—though in lesser numbers—all year long. And catalogs can sell your books. If you have a book of verse that is suitable for any of the specialty stores listed above, then you may appeal to shoppers browsing through specialty catalogs targeting the same market.

Where do the catalog companies get the items that they advertise? Many of the book items are bought from individual publishers who contact them, get the name of a buyer, and submit their product for consideration. In this case, your product is your book of poems.

I told you earlier about my friend who wrote the recipes in verse which he called the *Great Sweet Potato Cookbook*. Such a book, or another nostalgic one featuring family times and *Old Time Recipes from Grandma's Kitchen* might do well as an impulse item in kitchenware or gourmet catalogs. Here's how to research the catalog market:

- Save catalogs that might be compatible with your verse.
- Ask your friends to do the same.
- Check for other directories in the reference department of the largest public library near you.
- Search for "catalogs" on the internet, via Yahoo, etc.

- Call or write for a sample copy of any catalogs that may be of interest to you.
- When you find a catalog that you feel may be interested in your book, call to locate the appropriate buyer. Submit your book to that buyer, by name, for consideration.

Premium and Promotional Sales

There may be premium and promotional sales opportunities. In an earlier chapter, I mentioned the sale of a large quantity of copies of the collection of poems *Anson County* to the development office of that North Carolina county. *Key West Cats* could be given to customers by a small animal veterinary clinic. The *Great Sweet Potato Cookbook* is a natural for that segment of the agricultural industry.

I sold the entire first edition of my book *Tales of the Tobacco Country*—a folklore collection containing much verse—to the Philip Morris Tobacco Company, where it became an executive Christmas gift, distributed by the office of the president of the corporation.

Trust Your Hunches and Impulses

Your instincts and intuitions are your best friends. Act on them. When a marketing idea for your book occurs to you, act on it. You are a poet. Who are you to ignore messages from the universe? I can trace many of the best things that have happened to me to my willingness to act on an instinct or an impulse.

- When I was a student, I filled out an application for a Fulbright Fellowship on an impulse, sent it in, then forgot about it. Four months later I got a letter informing me that I was going to France for a year's study, all expenses paid, compliments of the Fulbright Commission.
- On an impulse, I dropped a tedious, traditional Ph.D. dissertation subject for a much more adventurous one on Mallarmé. I wrote it straight through, without revision, and it was accepted.
- On an impulse, I submitted that dissertation to the University of Georgia Press, without having any real reason to do so. As a result, my first book was accepted for publication.
- On an impulse, I sent a galley of an earlier version of this very

book to the Writer's Digest Book Club. I did it with a totally blind, "What-have-I-got-to-lose?" attitude. The book was accepted as an alternate selection, and I received an order for 1,500 copies.

When you have an idea that you feel might work for your book, act on it. It may just work for you. And there is one sure thing to consider: If you don't act, your idea can't possibly work.

Consignment Agreement

(Your name or the name of your publishing company) consigns ___ copies of (Title of book) to (Name of bookstore) for sale at a discount of _____%.

(Name of bookstore) agrees to display consigned copies and to pay to (Your name) ___ % of the retail price as the books are sold. Accountings will be made monthly, on the fifteenth of each month.

The period of this consignment will be from (date) to (date).

Unsold copies will be returned to (Your name) in good condition at the end of the agreed sales period.

Signed: _____

_____

Date: _____

This is the simple consignment agreement that I use. Something similar will work for you. Show this to your attorney for fine-tuning and review.

Chapter Thirteen /
A Poet's Guide to the Internet

Our tools shape our writing and publishing lives—the practical part of them, anyway. The act of writing itself, of creating something new out of our imaginations, is so difficult and demanding that any tool that will make any part of it easier is a great gift.

The invention of the mechanical typewriter was revolutionary. Even when writers chose to continue to write in longhand, manuscripts could be typed by others for ease of reading and editing. Fifty years later, the electric typewriter came along, followed by the self-correcting electric typewriter. When I bought my first IBM Selectric with its nifty little white-out ribbon in place, my life was greatly simplified. I was a fast but inaccurate typist. I saved an immense amount of time when I was able to self-correct typos in the final drafts of my manuscripts and, for the first time, routinely send out flawless query letters that I had to type only once.

Later, in 1985, I owned a $30,000 phototypesetter which I used to produce camera-ready copy for my books and magazines. It was a monster that broke down regularly. The maintenance agreement on it cost upwards of $5,000 a year. One year later, in 1986, I replaced that machine with a MacIntosh Plus and a Laserwriter. The Mac cost a fraction of the price of the phototypesetter, did a wholly adequate job, and never broke down. The MacIntosh on which I am writing this chapter is ten thousand times more powerful than that $30,000 behemoth. Furthermore, once I write a book, I simply import the word processing files into a page layout program to typeset them and lay them out.

The fax machine appeared in 1988. I held off buying one until I knew that the people with whom I did business would have one, too. That did not take long. In short order, not having a fax was a sign that you really weren't serious about doing business. Someone would ask, "What's your fax number?" You really couldn't afford to say, "I don't have one." It would make you sound like a piker. A few months later, my fax was working away, simplifying all my communications. I wondered what I had ever done without it.

And then came another tool, this one a real blockbuster.

Welcome to the Internet

In the early 1990's, I began to hear more and more about something called "the internet," but I had no idea what it really was. Then one day, I was helping write a campaign speech for a friend who was running for city council. We decided that we needed some census info, and I was about to walk over to the library to dig it out. Not necessary, my friend said. He took me upstairs to his office, booted up his computer, and logged onto Compuserve. Five minutes later we were looking at a count of every household and a profile of every demographic group in our county and town. A half day's work in half a minute. I was impressed.

Still, it was some time before I myself "went online." In the early days (eight or nine years ago) internet access could be expensive, and navigating the net was something of an esoteric experience: you had to deal with "gophers," "Veronicas," "Archies," and a host of other mysterious tools. The technical guys could understand it, but I just didn't have time to deal with the (then) lengthy learning curve. I was too busy writing.

The World Wide Web

But, like the fax machine, it was not too long before a new internet resource became a tool that I could not do without. That new resource was the development of the World Wide Web, whose "web pages" combined graphics and rich typographical resources. Furthermore, the web was totally geek-free, eliminating most of the technobabble that had baffled early, everyday users of the Internet. It was so easy to use, so simple in its operation, that even a child could manage it. This was in 1994. Today kids all over America sit in front of computer screens in library reference rooms, researching their term papers on the web.

The World Wide Web made the internet not only a source of information, but of information that was interesting to look at and easy to use. It also became a viable means of advertising, of marketing, of selling goods and services, of education, of informing, even of having fun. Today, "I found it on the web," and "You can find it on the web" have become commonplace expressions.

The Email Express

"I'll email you" has become commonplace, as well. Email is the most widely used feature of the internet. Allowing instant communication around the world, cost-free, email is truly a revolution. My web site, www.PubMart.com, sells how-to manuals on publishing magazines, weekly newspapers, and other periodicals. Yesterday, I got email orders from Portugal, Australia and Singapore. I received the orders just seconds after my customers placed them. I received a lawyer joke from my brother-in-law in Virginia. I had a note from my nephew in Savannah telling me that he had seen a mention of my publishing company, Venture Press, in *Entrepreneur* magazine. I had an email from a proofreader in Miami who is working on one of my manuscripts. I had twenty posts from a "mailing list" that I subscribe to—a group of small, independent publishers discussing the opportunities and pitfalls of the publishing business. I received the latest issues of two writers' newsletters that I enjoy and find very useful. I emailed the corrected proof of an article to my editor at *Home Office Computing* magazine.

You can't do without email today, any more than you could do without a telephone or a typewriter. Technophobe or not, if you don't have it, get it. Email will put you in instantaneous communication with the world. And that's something that even poets need.

Here are a few of the things that email will do for you:

- *News releases and public relations.* Your email program will allow you to keep a list of email addresses for editors, bookstore reading coordinators, and others to whom you wish to send news items and other announcements. Type your news release just once, click on the right button, and send it to all the news editors on your list. Email greatly simplifies your PR and business communication tasks and makes them more efficient and less expensive.

- *Writers' guidelines and queries.* More and more publications now disseminate writer's guidelines by email, and some now accept email queries. In the near future, all of them will do so. Query, negotiation, and submission of finished copy for a recent article of mine in *Home Office Computing* were handled entirely by email.

- *"Mailing lists" and discussion groups.* In internet parlance a "mailing list" is a group of individuals with shared interests who post email messages to the entire group. A list that I currently enjoy, for instance, is that of the Publisher's Marketing Association, an organization of small publishers. The publishing and marketing ideas that we exchange have been quite valuable to me.

- *Newsletters.* Many newsletters from writing and arts organizations are now distributed via email. (Indeed, you can do your own this way.) Email distribution does away with all costs of printing, stuffing of envelopes, and postage. I currently receive newsletters from the *Midwest Publisher's Association*, *The Rock*, and *Publishers Weekly* via email.

- *Personal communication.* And, of course, email simplifies your own personal communications immensely. Though you will still want to put pen to paper for special notes, email is perfectly acceptable for almost all other uses.

Surfing the Web

If email has become an essential tool for the writer, so has accessing the virtually unlimited resources of the internet. When I need a zip code, I can find in on the USPS site on the web. When my doctor prescribes a new drug, I can find all the research information I can possibly use on the web. When I need the email address of an editor or publisher, I can find it, within minutes, on the web. I was recently doing an article on creativity. A search led me to The Creativity Site, a vast body of resources and information on the subject. I make plane and hotel reservations on the web. I buy books and other products at steep discounts on the web.

Moreover, I keep up with my own profession via the web, accessing sites for poets, non-fiction writers, and fiction writers, as well as sites of professional organizations like the American Society of Journalists and Authors. I read *Publisher's Weekly*, the trade magazine of the publishing industry, on the web (a subscription for hard copy costs $129 year!). And all of this barely scratches the surface.

Find the "Supersites"

I could give you a list of scores of individual web sites for you to try one by one, but there is an easier way to get started: find the "supersites." Every web page has "links" to other web pages. Click on the link with your mouse, and you are immediately transported to that linked page. Supersites are web pages with very large numbers of links to other web sites dealing with the same subject matter.

Each supersite is a veritable catalog of resources. The web sites they list are usually pre-qualified for usefulness and are much more likely to be up and running than those you find listed individually and randomly. Web sites are being built and shut down every day. Printed lists, such as the Internet Yellow Pages and the appendices of books, are often largely out of date by the time they appear on the bookstore shelves. The supersites, on the other hand, are relatively stable and are updated regularly.

I have found the following supersites very useful in the field of writing and publishing. Pull them up and see where they lead you. Here are two of my favorites:

- The Midwest Book Review:
  http://www.midwestbookreview.com. Jim Cox, editor of the Midwest Book Review, does a fantastic job of assembling and constantly cleaning and updating his vast list of sites with writing-related content. Will save you many hours of research.

- Bookzone:
  http://www.bookzone.com. This site has hundreds of key links of interest to writers. I highly recommend it.

Your Own Web Page?

You can have your own home page at very little cost. Often a writers' club will put up a site on which members can post their own pages. I am a member of the National Writers' Association, South Florida Chapter. Our new web site is going up soon, and anyone who wants a spot on it can have it with no futher cost than the $30 a year dues that we already pay. I'll put up a page linking viewers with my business web site at www.PubMart.com. In the absence of a club, four or five friends can get together and put up a site for as little as four or five dollars a month each. Some sites offer free pages to writers. They may even help with design.

To design your own page, you will need a computer and a copy of a program like Frontpage (for Windows) or Adobe GoLive (for MacIntosh).Web design is a skill that is easily learned and that has a rich, long-term payoff.

You can use your web page to post your bio and credits, for public relations and publicity, and for other, similar purposes. When someone calls you about giving a reading or a talk, you can refer them to your web site for full information.

You can even become editor of your own electronic "webzine," although I personally consider the web more suitable for non-fiction and informational writing than for poetry. The look of the poem on the printed page is too important to me. But you could easily publish articles of interest to poets, book reviews, and news items about local happenings in the literary world. All-in-all, it can be quite an adventure.

Computer guru Peter Kent's book, *Poor Richard's Web Site* (Top Floor Publishing), is the very best of all the books out there. I have read dozens of them, and none is as easy to understand and as full of detailed how-to as this one. Kent says his book offers "Geek-free, Commonsense Advice on Building a Low-Cost Web Site," and he is 100% accurate. Look Peter Kent up at www.PoorRichard.com.

RECOMMENDED RESOURCE

There are many more than this, of course, and some of the sites listed below in the "reference and information" section could also qualify as supersites.

Reference and Information

There are basic, information-providing web sites of great value. The following list (just a sample) includes some that I use constantly. Such sites can be "bookmarked" in your web browser program so that you can get back to them at any time with a simple click of the mouse.

- Newspaper Association of America:
  http://newspaperlinks.com
  This site is a resource for locating email addresses of newspaper editors. I looked for such a site for a long time, and finally found this one by following a link from the Writers Center supersite. I looked up my local metropolitan paper, the *Miami Herald*. I clicked on the link in the NAA site and searched it by state, choosing Florida. The screen immediately showed a list of almost all the newspapers in Florida. I clicked on the *Miami Herald* and the home page of that newspaper opened up. There I found an internal link called "feedback." I clicked on that, and found the email address and telephone number of each department in the newspaper, from arts and leisure, to sports, to business. Such a site will help you build a very effective electronic mailing list for your email news releases. When

you are scheduled for a reading or a talk in another town, you can utilize this list to quickly send out news releases to the print media.

- The University of Pennsylvania library:
  http://www.library.upenn.edu/index.html
  The University of Pennsylvania library site focuses on internet journals and other electronic publications. It also provides links to the home pages of leading newspapers worldwide.

- The Library of Congress:
  http://www.loc.gov
  The Library of Congress site provides all the information you need to understand and apply for copyrights. You can even download the forms you need to fill out to register your copyright at http://www.lcweb.loc.gov/copyright.

- Bookwire:
  http://www.bookwire.com/
  Bookwire provides up-to-date news on the publishing industry, including links to *Publishers Weekly* and articles on major industry happenings, week-by-week.

- The Postal Service:
  http://www.usps.gov/ncsc/
  Need a zip code? Go to this site and enter the address. The code will appear in seconds.

- Writers Net:
  http://www.writers.net
  Among many other links, Writers Net provides names and addresses of editors and literary agents.

- Internet address finder:
  http://www.iaf.net/
  When you know a name, but need an internet address, go to

this site. It can often solve your problem for you.

- Judith Appelbaum's "How to Get Happily Published" site:
    http://www.happilypublished.com/links.html
    Judith Appelbaum established this site as a spin-off of her popular book of the same name. The site provides many tips and much valuable know-how from a true publishing professional.

- About.Com
    http://www.about.com
    Each About.Com site is devoted to a single topic—complete with site reviews, feature articles, and discussion areas—and each site is created by a qualified About.Com "guide," a company-certified subject specialist who's responsible for helping you get the most out of your time online. When they're not posting informative weekly features or combing the Net for fresh links to other useful online resources, many About.Com guides are hosting live chats, managing bulletin board discussions, recommending books, keeping abreast of relevant news, updating links, publishing newsletters, and responding to email. The guides really care about the topics they cover, and they're qualified to lead active online communities where you can always find reliable information and people who share your interests.

- National Endowment for the Arts:
    http://arts.endow.gov/
    This important site carries news of the availability and the awarding of grants to regional and local organizations, as well as addresses and links to local and regional web sites. Poets, more than any other writers, depend on grants to support their publishing activities. The NEA site should be regular reading for them.

- The American Society of Journalists and Authors:
    http://www.asja.org/

The World of the 'Zines

There are a number of "magazines" which are posted on the internet, accessible only electronically. These are referred to as "webzines" or "ezines," and there is a distinction to make between them, although it is often blurred. The word "webzine" is theoretically reserved for free publications which can be pulled up by anybody. "Ezines," on the other hand, charge a subscription fee and, after a sample copy, are read only by paying customers. Although these two labels are not always used accurately, the two types of electronic magazine do indeed exist.

Ephemeral ezines and webzines rise to the surface and sink again every day, so ezine land has an ever-changing landscape. And an ever-changing cast of characters, too. Because they are so easy and so inexpensive to launch, many are more like personal fiefdoms than anything else— undisciplined, eccentric, and often downright bizarre. Few are truly distinguished.

The truth, it seems to me, is that the marriage of computer screens and poetry (or short stories or novels) is definitely not a match made in heaven. Serious writers use the internet as a more and more indispensable medium for the exchange of information and ideas, but not for publication of their work. When such writers do post their work it is usually as a participant in a critique group or workshop

Although the members of ASJA are mainly writers of non-fiction, this site is of considerable interest to all other writers as well. Especially interesting is its "contract watch," which reports on contract disputes between authors and publications. Its goal is to promote and protect the work of all writers.

- Poetry Society of America:
  http://www.poetrysociety.org/
  This is one of the oldest literary organizations in the United States, having been founded in the late nineteenth century. The site contains much information and many links of interest to poets, and is of the highest quality.

- Poets & Writers Online
  http://www.pw.org/
  Elsewhere in this book, I suggested that you subscribe to *Poets & Writers* magazine, which I consider the very best publication available for the literary writer of both poetry and prose. Now that magazine has a web site which extends its fine work to the web. Highly recommended.

- Writer's Digest
  http://www.writersdigest.com
  Readers of *Writer's Digest* will be glad to know that the magazine now has a web site to disseminate information to all writers of poetry, non-fiction, and fiction. There is much useful information in *Writer's Digest*, but beware of its advertisements for poetry contests, many of which are of questionable value.

This brief list is the merest beginning to finding internet resources for poets. I list these particular sites for two reasons. First, over the years that I have been utilizing the internet these are some of the best and most useful resources that I have found. They represent the results of many hours of traveling about the web, looking, testing, prodding, and poking until I came up with some really substantial material. Second, I want to tempt all of my readers to try the web out. You might as well get ahead of the game. Why play catch-up on the use of this revolutionary tool?

Appendix I: Contacts and Sources

The books listed below are carefully selected from the hundreds of titles available. Each of them has been a valuable source of information to me on writing and publishing. Each contains concrete, usable information and techniques to help you reach your goals, both literary and entrepreneurial. (Yes, even a chapbook publisher is an entrepreneur!) I highly recommend them to you.

Since many of these books exist in a variety of editions, some expensive and some much less expensive, I suggest that you consult *Books in Print* and *Paperback Books in Print* at your library or bookstore to find the one that best fits your needs and pocketbook. If funds are in short supply, check out your local library. If the books aren't on the shelf, ask your librarian to get them for you through interlibrary loan. A few are very expensive (in the $110-200 range) and can be consulted in the reference room of most large public libraries, although not always in the latest edition. Libraries have budget problems, too.

Books on Writing and Publishing

Appelbaum, Judith. *How to Get Happily Published.* Harper-Collins. Fifth Edition. A friendly guide to the world of publishing for those who know little about it. Techniques for approaching traditional publishers, as well as an introduction to alternative self-publishing. A problem solver, too. When someone asks, "I've written a book. How do I get it published?" you can answer, "Read Judith Appelbaum's book. It's all in there."

Author & Audience: A Readings and Workshops Guide. Poets & Writers, Inc. A guide to the presentation of readings and workshops nationwide. Contains a valuable contact list of sponsoring groups.

Balkin, Richard. *A Writer's Guide to Book Publishing.* Dutton Books. 1981. Written from the writer's perspective, Balkin's book is a primer on the business side of publishing. There is a useful and thorough discussion of book publishing contracts, though the agreements that Balkan discusses are far more complicated than those that will be needed to carry out the projects outlined in *Poet Power!*

Barker, Malcolm E. *Book Design and Production for the Small Publisher.* Londonborn Publications. This is an easy-to-read-and-use guide to creating handsome books. Recommended for self-publishers and publishers of a chapbook series.

Brabec, Barbara. *Homemade Money.* Betterway Publications. 5th Edition. 1994. Barbara Brabec's book is a gentle but very useful introduction to running a small, sideline enterprise from your own home. *Homemade Money* will reassure nervous publishers and sellers of their own poetry and that of others that "doing business" is not really as scary as it sounds and can even be a lot of fun.

Brande, Dorothea. *Becoming a Writer.* Jeremy P. Tarcher, Inc. Brande's little book, as well as one or two others that she has written, contains insights that, without exaggeration, can free you to be the writer you want to be. I came across her books by accident, while browsing the shelves in a small-town library. It was one of the happiest accidents of my life. There is a mountain of advice out there, but not much of it really works, as Brande's does.

Cook, James R. *The Start-Up Entrepreneur.* E. P. Dutton, 1989. This is a solid, common sense look at the pleasures and perils of going into business for yourself. It will be very useful for any of you who are considering going into publishing in a serious way, publishing your own poetry series and maybe even a literary magazine or two.

Haldeman-Julius, Emmanuel. *The First Hundred Million*. Arno Press. 1974. In *The First Hundred Million*, newspaperman-publisher Haldeman-Julius tells the fascinating story of the creation of his "Little Blue Book" series. The Blue Books were simple, saddle-stitched pamphlets containing reprints of the classics, as well as practical information on such then-taboo topics as sex education for women. Anyone interested in the publishing and book world should treat themselves to a read of this book. There is a great chapter on Haldeman-Julius's "Book Hospital," to which he consigned books that weren't selling well, tinkered with the title, and transformed them into profitable publications. If you don't think the choice of a title is important, this chapter will change your mind. This chapter is also available on my web site at www.PubMart.com.

Henderson, Bill. *The Publish-It-Yourself Handbook*. Harper & Row, 1987. Henderson's book presents a dozen or more essays by literary writers and poets telling how they took charge of their own careers and published their own work and, often, the works of others. Inspiring and reassuring. You really ought to read it.

Hurlburt, Alan. *The Grid*. National Composition Association. Hurlburt explains the grid system of design and layout. It works like magic for brochures, catalogs, magazines, and other publications. I found it very valuable, as it allowed me, in the days before I had any experience in design, to do reasonably good work.

Jerome, Judson. *The Poet's Handbook*. Writer's Digest Books. The late Judson Jerome packed good sense and useful advice into his Writer's Digest columns over a period of many years. This collection makes Jerome's ideas available in book form. Highly recommended.

Kamoroff, Bernard. *Small-Time Operator: How to Start Your Own Small Business, Keep Your Books, Pay Your Taxes, & Stay Out of Trouble!* Bell Springs Publishing. If you are a writer sending work out to magazines and book publishers, or if you are publishing your own work, you are in business. Kamaroff tells you how to handle all the records that you need to keep. Very clear, and written for the accounting-impaired—that is, for people like me. This book is one of the great self-publishing success stories, by the way. Published by Kamaroff himself, it has been on bookstore shelves for years and through many editions.

Kremer, John. *1001 Ways to Market Your Books.* Open Horizons. 1998. Kremer's book is a great idea-generator. When sales on one of my books are languishing, I browse through Kremer. Almost always, I will discover an avenue I haven't explored, or something Kremer says will bring another, related idea to mind. An excellent resource for anyone selling books.

A Manual of Style for Authors, Editors and Copywriters (Chicago Style Book). University of Chicago Press. This utterly complete handbook is as close to an industry standard as any. It should be on every writer's bookshelf. Academic (scholarly) writers may prefer the *Modern Language Association Stylebook*, and social scientists sometimes prefer the *American Psychological Association Stylebook*. The Chicago manual is the big one, and the most generally accepted.

Moyer, Page Emory. *The ABC's of a Really Good Speech*. Circle Press. While a poetry reading or seminar is not really a "speech," you can learn a great deal from Moyer's book about connecting with the audience in an effective way, something many writers who give presentations need to work hard on.

Parker, Roger C. *Looking Good in Print: A Guide to Basic Design for Desktop Publishing*. Ventana Press. Through each of its three editions, Parker's book has become a standard resource for publication designers. Great for your media kit and promotional material design.

Poynter, Dan. *The Self Publishing Manual*. Para Publishing. A thorough introduction to the self-publication and marketing of adult non-fiction. Much of the information is also of use to literary publishers.

Rice, Stanley. *Book Design* (2 vols.). R.R. Bowker. These two slim volumes are the only source of complete book design information that I have been able to find. Very usable and easy to understand. A thorough discussion of the rules of the game.

Romano, Frank. *Practical Typography from A to Z*. National Composition Association. Made up of easy-to-use alphabetical entries, this small book contains almost everything you need to know about type specifications. One entry, for instance, deals very clearly with the relationship between type size, leading and line length. Misunderstanding these factors can lead to the creation of unnecessarily hard to read pages.

White, Jan V. *Editing by Design*. R.R. Bowker. 1985. A classic in publication design, White's book is especially good in its discussion of the relationship between text and art.

A Writer's Guide to Copyright. Poets & Writers, Inc. It may be hard to believe, but few writers are really familiar with copyright law. This book will tell you what you want (and need) to know.

Marketing and Promotion

There are many books on promotion and publicity. The following are among the best. Although there will be some duplication of ideas among them, each contains ideas and strategies not found in the others. And when one such idea works for you in your effort to sell your book, it is worth all the reading and research you have done to find it.

Caples, John. *Tested Advertising Methods*. Fred E. Hahn. If you want to know what makes advertising work, read John Caples's book. It is a classic in the field. Caples learned the art of selling through his work in the mail order business. He learned what worked and what didn't by a simple means: if he wrote a bad ad, there were no orders. A good ad brought in profitable replies. His analysis of hundreds of such ads give us all valuable insight into writing effective promotional material and advertisements.

Feldman, Elaine. *The Writer's Guide to Self-Promotion & Publicity.* Writer's Digest Books. Publishing companies have "publicists" who promote their books for them. Poets have to promote their own books and be their own publicists. Feldman's book tells how it can be done.

Fletcher, Tana, and Julia Rockler. *Getting Publicity: A Do-it-Yourself Guide for Small Business and Non-Profit Groups.* Self-Counsel Press. Good on tips for those in literary publishing and the arts.

Glenn, Peggy. *Publicity for Books and Authors: A Do-It-Yourself Handbook for Small Publishing Firms and Enterprising Authors.* Aames-Allen Publishing Co. I found Peggy Glenn especially helpful in her chapters on dealing with radio and TV public relations and promotion.

O'Keefe, Steve. *Publicity on the Internet.* John Wiley & Sons. Steve O'Keefe has written a fine book, filled-to-bursting with how-to information on the distribution of public relations, advertising, and promotional material via the internet. For an introduction to this new frontier, read O'Keefe's book.

Playle, Ron. *Selling to Catalog Houses.* Playle Publications, Inc., P.O. Box 778, Des Moines, IA 80303. 1989. The catalog game, and how it is played. How to submit your book to catalogs for purchase and resale.

Appendix I

Organizations and Networking

It is stimulating to meet others interested in the same things that interest you and exchange ideas, information, and news of opportunities. In attending local meetings or in reading the newsletters of national organizations, you will hear about or read about new magazines, new publishers, new foundations, grant opportunities, writers' conferences, literary competitions, job opportunities, and more.

Local Clubs and Organizations. Networking begins at home. If you live in New York, Los Angeles, or San Francisco, "local" can also mean "national." But in every town of any size there are writers' and poets' guilds, clubs, and associations. They offer everything from moral support to publication opportunities and everything in between: writers' conferences, critique groups, workshops, and competitions. Until very recently, I lived in Coral Springs, a suburb of Fort Lauderdale, Florida. Just to the north were the Palm Beach Writer's Guild and the Poets of the Palm Beaches club. In Miami, to the south, I found the National Writer's Association, South Florida Chapter. There was the Palm Beach Book Fest in the spring and the Miami Book Fair in the fall, both of which drew—and still draw—name novelists, poets, dramatists and journalists, both as speakers and attendees. In North Carolina, where I lived before moving to Florida, there was the state-wide North Carolina Writers Network, with its headquarters in the Chapel Hill-Carrboro area, as well as writers' clubs in the towns where I lived. Look up your local clubs. Membership is usually open to anyone interested in writing and publishing.

The Authors Guild, Inc., 330 West 42 Street, New York, NY 10036; 212-563-5904; fax: 212-564-5363. Two important national organizations for writers are the American Society of Journalists and Authors and The Authors Guild. The ASJA is open only to nonfiction writers with proven track records of publication. The Authors Guild membership includes novelists and poets. The Guild has a newsletter and acts as an author's advocate in setting publishing community standards.

Authors Unlimited, 31 East 32 Street, Suite 300, New York, NY 10016. This is a literary speakers bureau. Once you have established a name for yourself and developed a presentation that will appeal to a wide variety of listeners, you may want to register with Authors Unlimited. Write for their guidelines.

CLMP (Council of Literary Magazines and Presses) , 154 Christopher Street, Suite 3C, New York, NY 10014; 212-741-9110; fax: 212-741-9112. This organization is devoted to the interests of literary writers and, especially, publishers.

Finally, I recommend that you write the following two organizations to request brochures describing their resources and services, and ask to be put on their mailing lists. The first is the *Small Press Center*, 20 W. 44 Street, New York, NY 10036; 212-764-7021. The second is *Poets & Writers, Inc.* 72 Spring Street, New York, NY 10012; 212 226-3586.

Directories and Guides

American Book Trade Directory. R. R. Bowker, 121 Chanlon Road, New Providence, NJ 07974. Lists of bookstores and retail outlets, along with distributors and wholesalers.

American Library Directory. R. R. Bowker, 121 Chanlon Road, New Providence, NJ 07974. Public and school libraries. Each entry also indicates the monies allotted for new purchases.

Bacon's Publicity Checker. Bacon's, 332 South Michigan Avenue, Chicago, IL 60604. Updated annually.

Bacon's Radio/TV Directory. Bacon's, 332 South Michigan Avenue, Chicago, IL 60604. Updated annually.

Contemporary Authors. Gale Research Inc., P.O. Box 33477, Detroit, MI 48232-3477. Once you have published, you can get listed here. Write for the form you will need.

A Directory of American Poets and Fiction Writers. Poets & Writers, Inc., 72 Spring Street, New York, NY 10012. 6,000-plus names and addresses of leading literary authors.

The Directory of Mail Order Catalogs. Richard Gottlieb, Editor. Grey House Publishing, Pocket Knife Square, Lakeville, CT 06039. Research source for catalog sales.

Directory of Poetry Publishers. Dustbooks, P.O. Box 100, Paradise, CA 95967; 800-477-6110. This directory lists magazines and publishers who are receptive to poetry and literary manuscripts. These publications come and go with alarming speed, so consult the latest edition to get the most nearly correct address.

The Foundation Center, 79 Fifth Avenue, New York, NY 10003-3050; 212-620-4230. There are regional offices at 1001 Connecticut Avenue, NW, Suite 938, Washington, DC 20036, at 312 Sutter Street, San Francisco, CA 94108, and at 1356 Hanna Building, 1422 Euclid Avenue, Cleveland, OH 44115. Contact the Foundation Center for information on grants for writers.

Gale Directory of Publications and Broadcast Media. Edited by Karen E. Koek and Julie Winklepleck. Gale Research Inc, P.O. Box 33477, Detroit, MI 48232-3477. Names and addresses of print and electronic media.

Gebbie's All-In-One Directory. Gebbie Press. This is an easy-to-use directory of magazines, newspapers and radio and TV stations. It is also available as an electronic mailing list. You can get the information you need at http://www.gebbie.com.

The International Directory of Little Magazines and Small Presses. Dustbooks, P.O. Box 100, Paradise, CA 95967; 800-477-6110.

Literary Market Place. R.R. Bowker, 121 Chanlon Road, New Providence, NJ 07974. Updated annually. Usually referred to simply as "LMP," *Literary Market Place* is the most complete directory of all persons and organizations associated with the publishing business: publishing houses and their specialties, editors, agents, book clubs, manufacturers, suppliers, etc. A new edition is published each year. While street addresses may not change rapidly, the names of editors do. Always use the latest issue available to you.

The National Directory of Catalogs. Matthew Manning, Fay Shapiro, and Frank Renkiewicz, eds. Oxbridge Communications, Inc., 150 Fifth Avenue, New York, NY 10011 (paper). This is an expensive ($150), but useful, resource for exploring the catalog market for your books. You will probably want to consult it in the reference room of your library.

Poet's Market: Where & How to Publish Your Poetry. Writer's Digest Books, 1807 Dana Avenue, Cincinnati, OH 48207. Published yearly.

Publisher's Directory. Edited by Thomas M. Bachmann. Gale Research Inc. P.O. Box 33477, Detroit, MI 48232-3477. This resource lists small and specialty publishers.

Publication Grants for Writers & Publishers. Oryx Press, 4041 North Central at Indian School Road, Phoenix, AZ 85012-3397. 1991. This manual tells you how to write and submit proposals for grants.

Magazines and Newsletters

American Bookseller. American Booksellers Association, 860 White Plains Road, Tarrytown, NY 10891; 800-637-0037. Published monthly. Read this one in the library and keep up with bookstore trends, what's selling and what's not, bookstore needs and problems. Knowing these things will give you some insight into bookstore concerns when you approach them about selling your book or giving a reading.

American Poetry Review. 1721 Walnut Street, Philadelphia, PA 19103. Published bimonthly.

Foreword Magazine. This magazine focuses on the world of independent and small press publishing. *Foreword* is a good place to send your books for review. The magazine has a controlled circulation of 20,000.

Independent Publisher. This magazine has led a checkered existence since it was founded twenty or so years ago by R.R. Bowker as *Small Press Magazine*. The current version has fairly limited circulation, but it does focus on small and literary publishers, and it is interested in seeing your books for possible review.

Poets and Writers Magazine. Poets & Writers, Inc., 72 Spring Street, New York, NY 10012. Published bimonthly. The best of all magazines for poets and literary authors. Brilliantly edited. Not only a great read, but useful, too.

Publisher's Weekly. PW, as it is called, is the trade magazine of the big-time publishing industry. If you are interested in the business of books, subscribe for a year and try it out. Or go to the PW web site (at Bookwire). See chapter 13 for directions.

The Writer. The Writer, Inc., 120 Boylston Street, Boston, MA 02116-4615. Published monthly. An old-timer in the field, the magazine deals mostly with fiction through articles on the craft written by authors who have made it.

Writer's Digest. Probably the most widely-read magazine for writers, *Writer's Digest* has something of a split personality, combining useful articles on the craft with large numbers of advertisements for "editorial services" and "poetry contests" that one would do well to check out before deciding to participate in them.

Appendix II / Glossary of Book Design, Printing, and Publishing Terms

"AA"

Abbreviation for author's alteration. Any change made by the customer after initial typography is done. Such alterations result in additional charges to the author.

alignment

Orientation of type with regard to edges of the column or paper, such as aligned right (flush right), aligned left (flush left), and aligned on center (centered).

author's alterations

See "AA," above.

back matter

Appendices, index, author bio, order form and other materials which may be included in the back of a book.

backup copy

Second copy of any book or manuscript carefully kept safe in the event the first copy is lost or damaged.

bar code

Printed on the back cover of a book. Includes publisher ID, International Standard Book Number and sometimes price. Most bookstores require bar codes. Cashiers scan them for price and inventory control.

bleed

When printing (or background color) extends to the very edge of the page it is said to "bleed." Such printing is referred to as "a bleed."

blueline
> Photographic proof made from negatives which will be used to etch printing plates. Also referred to as "blues." This is the publisher's last chance to check for errors, although by this late stage of production, it is hoped that all corrections will have been made.

blurb
> Among other uses, a quote of praise or endorsement usually appearing on the back cover of a book.

bold type
> Type that appears darker than ordinary type of the same typeface. The main word entries in the glossary are set in bold type.

book paper
> Also referred to as "text stock." Category of paper suitable for publication printing.

bullet
> Bold dot often placed before each item in a list to set it off from the other items.

C1S
> Coated on one side. Cover stock that is coated (has a gloss) on one side only.

camera-ready copy
> Pages of a book or other publication that are ready for the printer to use to make negatives and plates.

cataloging in publication data
> Library of Congress cataloging data usually printed on the copyright page to assist librarians in cataloging a book. Not necessary for books of poetry.

change order
> A change in the original specifications for a book or other publication. Change orders should always be in writing.

character
> Any letter, numeral, punctuation mark, or other alphanumeric symbol.

clip art
> Drawings available for purchase for unlimited reproduction. Clip art is in the public domain. Clip art collections may be purchased in printed form or on computer disks.

color separation
> Film negative for printing color. One film negative is needed for each color. To print a "full color" photograph, four pieces of film are necessary, one for each primary color: cyan, magenta, yellow, and black.

continuous-tone copy
> All photographs and those illustrations having a range of shades. Contrasted with "line art," which is pure black and white.

copy
> 1) For an editor or typesetter, all written material. 2) For a graphic designer or printer, everything to be printed: art, photographs, and graphics, as well as words.

copy editor
> Person who checks and corrects a manuscript for spelling, grammar, punctuation, inconsistencies, inaccuracies, and conformity to style requirements. Also called line editor. The copy editor is not the same as a proofreader, who checks only for typographical and other mechanical errors.

copyright
> Certification of ownership of a work by a writer, photographer, artist, or organization. Notice of copyright is normally printed on the verso of the title page in books.

copyright notice
>   Statement of the date of copyright and the person or organization owning the copyright.

dash
>   Typographic mark that indicates a break between thoughts. An em dash (—) is longer than an en dash (–) and much longer than a hyphen (-).

desktop publishing
>   Term invented by Apple Computer in the mid-1980's to describe the revolutionary typesetting and graphic arts capabilities of their new MacIntosh computer and laser printer. Now extended to all such devices.

dingbat
>   Typographic symbol, such as a bullet (•), used for emphasis or decoration.

display type
>   Type used for headlines, advertising, and signs.

dropped cap
>   Large capital letter that extends down into the first two or more lines. Used as a design element.

edition
>   All the books sharing the same textual content. When you go back to press for additional books, this is called a second printing. If you add or subtract significant material, the new books are called a second edition.

fair use
>   Provision of the copyright law that allows short quotations from a copyrighted product to be used without permission of the copyright holder.

feature article
>Newspaper article that reads more like a magazine article, as distinguished from a news article.

filler
>Short items used to fill small blank spaces in a layout. Short, humorous verse can be used as filler.

fixed costs
>Costs incurred before the press starts running, which remain the same no matter how many or how few copies of your book are printed

flush left
>Type aligned along the left edge only. Also called left justified and ragged right. See the following example:

>Mary had a little lamb,
>Its fleece was white as snow.
>And everywhere that Mary went
>The lamb was sure to go.

flush right
>Type aligned along the right side of the column only. Also called right justified and ragged left. See the following example:

>Mary had a little lamb,
>Its fleece was white as snow.
>And everywhere that Mary went
>The lamb was sure to go.

folio
>Term used to designate the page number.

font
>A typeface family and all its characters and symbols.

footer
>Information, such as page number or chapter title, that appears regularly at the bottom of every page; running foot.

format
>Trim size or chosen page design of a book.

front matter
>Title page, copyright, dedication, etc. All pages in a book appearing before the actual text begins.

frontispiece
>Illustration or photograph appearing opposite the title page.

galley (galleys)
>Preliminary proofs of actual pages. "Bound galleys" are often sent out for review or comment before the actual print run of finished copies.

halftone
>A black and white photograph, as it appears in a printed book.

hard copy
>Pages printed on paper.

imprint
>The name of the publisher as it appears on the title page. Publishing companies have multiple imprints.

ISBN
>International Standard Book Number, abbreviated as ISBN. Every book published needs one of these, obtained from the R. R. Bowker Company. When you have an ISBN you will be listed in *Books In Print*, the chief national database of published works.

italic type
>Type slanted to the right to resemble handwriting, as compared to roman type. *This sentence is set in italic type.*

justified type

Type set flush right and left. See the example below:

> What is mysticism? Everyone knows and no one knows. According to the widest range of historical testimony, the mystical experience is ineffable. One hears, one sees, one knows, but one cannot tell.

kern

To reduce space between characters so those characters appear better fitted together.

leading

The distance between the baseline of two succeeding lines of type, measured in "points."

mark up

Instructions written on a manuscript to let the typographer know the font, size, leading, etc. to use.

markup

The difference between the wholesale price and the retail price.

masthead

Block of information in a publication that lists publishing, production, and editorial staffs, and gives address and telephone numbers for key departments.

overrun

Number of books printed in excess of the quantity ordered. Overruns and underruns occur because it is impossible for the printer to know how many books will be spoiled in the printing and binding process.

page proof

Proof of type and graphics as they will look on the finished page, complete with elements such as headings and rules.

perfect bind
> Binding method where pages are glued into a cover, squared off at the spine.

PMS
> PANTONE Matching System, used to specify color.

point
> The unit of measure expressing the size of type and leading.

point of purchase display (POP)
> Rack which contains books for display near the cash register. Especially effective and necessary for chapbooks and thin books of poetry.

ppi
> Pages per inch. All text stock has a ppi rating. This rating allows the designer to calculate the thickness of the finished book.

prepress
> All of the work performed to ready a book for publication.

proofread
> To read a manuscript to detect errors in spelling, grammar, and typesetting. Proofreading is a skill that many writers, though thoroughly familiar with the rules of grammar and orthography, do not possess.

proofreader marks
> Standard symbols and abbreviations used to correct manuscripts and proofs.

publisher
> CEO or owner of a publishing company. When you self-publish, you become the CEO of your own publishing company.

quote (printer's)
> This is a firm price, in writing, for the production of a book based on your specifications.

reverse
> Type reproduced by printing ink around its outline, leaving the color of the paper beneath to form the letters.

RFQ
> A request for quote. An RFQ form is reproduced earlier in this book.

saddle-stitch
> A binding method whereby pages are stapled together on the spine. See illustration below:

staples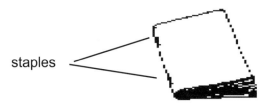

sans serif type
> Type without serifs. Also called gothic type.

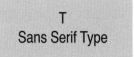

T
Sans Serif Type

screen
> Convert a photograph to a printed halftone.

serif
> Type with serifs; a decorative line at the ends of the type character.

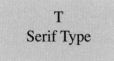

T
Serif Type

sidebar
>Short segment of information related to the text but set off from it in some way. There are many sidebars in this book, shaded in gray and in a different, contrasting font.

signature
>When a single sheet of paper goes through a printing press it will have eight, sixteen or even thirty-two pages of your book on it. This sheet is then folded so that the pages appear in order. All the pages on a single sheet constitute a "signature."

specifications
>Complete technical description of the work to be done, whether for typesetting or printing. See the request for quote form reproduced earlier in this book.

terms and conditions
>Specific details of a contract with typographer or a printer.

trade customs
>The trade customs of the printing industry, usually listed in small print on the reverse side of a quote or contract, are included in the terms and conditions of any agreement with a printer. Read these carefully. If any don't meet with your approval, you can cross them out and initial them, but your printer will have to agree with the changes

trim size
>The final trimmed dimensions of the pages in a publication.

typeface
>See font, above. A font is a type family. A typeface refers to any members of that family.

type family
>A group of related typefaces with the same name, such as Times roman, Times italic, Times roman bold, and Times bold italic.

type size
> The height of a typeface, measured from the top of the ascenders (i.e., the stem of an "h") to the bottom of the descenders (i.e., the tail of a "g").

type style
> Refers to the member of the type family chosen, such as roman (also called plain), italic, or bold.

typography
> The art of setting type. Also refers to the look of type on the page.

underrun
> Quantity of printing delivered that is less than the quantity ordered. Underruns are permitted under the trade customs of the printing industry. If this is not agreeable to you, specify "no unders."

unit cost
> Divide the total cost of a printing job by the number of units produced to get a cost per unit.

variable costs
> Printing costs that vary with the number of books printed. As distinguished from "fixed costs," above.

work for hire
> Ordinarily, creative works are the intellectual property of the creator. However, when explicitly agreed to by contract, the work becomes the intellectual property of the party specified in the contract, usually the person or organization paying for the creation of the work.

Index

Index

Index

About the Author

Thomas A. Williams, Ph.D., has written for magazines ranging from *Esquire* to *Writer's Digest*. The author of fourteen books, Williams is comfortable on both sides of the editorial desk. In addition to his free-lance writing, Tom Williams has started, edited, and published city and regional magazines and is currently Editor-in-Chief of Venture Press, book publishers.

In 1979, Williams bought The Mecklenburg Gazette, a weekly newspaper in North Carolina. In three years, he increased circulation 400 percent and revenues by 1,000 percent, and sold out to a newspaper chain for fifty times the purchase price.

Subsequently, Williams founded Venture Press, a home-based book publishing company. The Venture Press list includes how-to books and eBooks for writers and publishers, historical reprints, civic histories, folklore, oral history and poetry.

He has started and published many magazines, including *Tar Heel: The Magazine of North Carolina* (a state-wide magazine), *The New East, NC East*, and other regional, consumer magazines. He published association directories, chamber of commerce "quality of life" magazines, newcomer guides, and tourism guides.

Williams is a student of hard knocks. He learned how to position his publications for success on his own and shares his knowledge with us in his books. You can contact Tom Williams through his web site at www.PubMart.Com.

Sentient Publications, LLC publishes books on cultural creativity, experimental education, transformative spirituality, holistic health, new science, ecology, and other topics, approached from an integral viewpoint. Our authors are intensely interested in exploring the nature of life from fresh perspectives, addressing life's great questions, and fostering the full expression of the human potential. Sentient Publications' books arise from the spirit of inquiry and the richness of the inherent dialogue between writer and reader.

Our Culture Tools series is designed to give social catalyzers and cultural entrepreneurs the essential information, technology, and inspiration to forge a sustainable, creative, and compassionate world.

We are very interested in hearing from our readers. To direct suggestions or comments to us, or to be added to our mailing list, please contact:

SENTIENT PUBLICATIONS, LLC
1113 Spruce Street
Boulder, CO 80302
303-443-2188
contact@sentientpublications.com
www.sentientpublications.com